AF574426

PURITY & PASSION

RICK GHENT, M.A.
JIM CHILDERSTON, Ph.D.

GARY J. OLIVER, Ph.D.,
GENERAL EDITOR

MOODY PRESS
CHICAGO

ISBN 0-8024-7130-7

1 3 5 7 9 10 8 6 4 2

Printed in the United States of America

To my wife, Karen, who knows me as well as I know myself
and yet continues to love me

To my children, Rachael and Raleigh;
if they lined up all the children in the world
to pick from, I would pick the two of you

To my friends Carl and Tom;
I love you guys

To Carolyn, with love and appreciation
for encouraging me to continue pursuing intimacy
even when it's work or painful

CONTENTS

SEXUAL INSIGHTS

ACKNOWLEDGMENTS

The authors are grateful to Gary J. Oliver, the general editor of the Men of Integrity series, for the opportunity to write this book as well as his encouragement. We also appreciate the skilled insights of Larry Weeden in making this book authentic and down to earth. Larry's writing style and insights helped us bring the text to life.

We are not always as objective as we would like in evaluating the manuscript, and two people have helped us in critiquing our work. I (Rick) thank Kathy DeAnda for her dedicated effort to guide my writing skills and focus my direction. I (Jim) thank Carolyn Goltz, who typed much of the manuscript and also gave an honest, helpful critique of my material. Her creativity, insight, openness, and encouragement throughout this project was invaluable.

Finally, we are grateful to Jim Bell, Moody Press editorial director, and Jim Vincent, our editor, for helping refine our ideas and believing in us as writers. Thanks for your confidence in us.

1

SEX IS GREAT

If you're like me (Rick), you think sex is great. Would it surprise you if I said that God agrees? The fact is, He invented the whole deal. But if God thought sex up and it's so great, why is it so hard to figure out? I have tried to do that for years. I've also tried to figure out my wife. I ask myself questions like these: How does God fit into my sex life? Why have I felt so guilty about fantasies? When does a fantasy become lust? Is my sex life normal? Do I have sex often enough? How do I get my wife to want and enjoy sex more?

It's great to be a man. Sometimes, however, I'm made to feel as if being a man is a crime; some of my friends feel the same way. My friend John attended a marriage conference and came back shaking his head. "I got the message that the problem in most marriages is the man," he told me. "It's like marriage would be great if men were not part of the picture. We men get a bad rap when it comes to marriage.

"I want my wife to feel loved. I want to be loved by my wife. I want to be accepted and understood just like she does. I'm not an insensitive jerk. I don't always know how to do marriage, but I want our marriage to be good."

We men want to enjoy marriage and sex. And if you're a single man, you want to be comfortable with your sexuality too. You want to know how you can express it, and how to channel it to be honest and whole. Jim and I don't have all the answers. We wish men didn't have to struggle with expressing their sexuality. The facts are, however, that we men do have problems with sex, and sex is complicated.

Jim and I have laughed a lot as we talked about this book. "Who are we to help men with their sexuality?" one part of us asks. We've struggled like every other guy when it comes to sex. Jim told me, "While growing up, I would sit in church writing sexual words in the hymnal. I was bored and found my mind floating. I did not mean to offend God, of course. I was just a kid having fun." And I must admit at one point I liked to steal *Playboy* magazine from the local supermarket. As a budding teen in a stage of curiosity and rebellion, I did it for something to do; I quickly grew out of it. Now as an adult I continue to fight lust, and I reckon I always will. So are we experts? We continue to counsel men, both married and single, about the sexual issues of their lives, and we had the training, so I guess we're qualified. But like all men, we recognize that we are not always comfortable in our sexuality.

We have been reading the books on spirituality and sexuality. When we first sat down to write this book, we wanted to title it *Spiritual Sexuality.* We almost wrote a great theological work to fit that title. But let's face it—most married men could give a rip about a mystical experience in sex. We just want sex to be great, not miraculous. And single men want to be comfortable with their sexuality and know how to deal with their sexual feelings and urges.

Most of the men I see as a counselor, however, need help with sexual issues. Most of us have expectations of sex that are not being met. And most of us exaggerate how often we do have sex. A lot of men are addicted to sex. That includes a lot of single men, many of whom are sexually active even though they're Christians. Although the majority of married men are faithful to their wives and committed to marriage, a lot of them are having affairs. What's amazing is that even those men desire strong marriages. And most men would like to talk to friends about our struggles, yet they feel it would look foolish to bring up those struggles. For all these reasons, Jim and I are convinced that a book like this is desperately needed.

An Honest Man

A couple of years back, I was on a great mountain bike ride with my friend Greg. We have been friends for more than ten years and have a very open friendship, but we seldom talked about our sex lives. We were riding with our wives in the beautiful mountains of Colorado. Greg and I rode on ahead, as men like to do when they ride mountain bikes. When we got to the top of one pass, we pulled over to wait for our wives.

As we waited, Greg began to open up about some struggles in the sexual area. He was being incredibly honest. At first we both felt a bit strange talking about sex. But whom do you talk about your sex life with if not one of your closest friends?

Greg began, "I feel like my wife is no longer interested in sex."

I admitted I had similar feelings—in fact, I wondered if my wife had ever really been interested enough.

Then we discussed the need to talk to our wives about our sex lives. Greg wasn't so sure about that idea. "Talking to my wife about our sex life feels like a strange thing to do," he said. "Surely she should know my needs and desire sex. Don't you think talking to our wives would take love out of the picture?"

I had been to graduate school in counseling, so "of course" I knew the answers. "We don't need to be afraid to discuss these issues with our wives," I said. "That would only create intimacy."

So why was I so afraid to do it myself? Why was Greg so cautious about expressing his true feelings to his wife? The answer is that we wanted sex to work without the hassles of talking about it. We were hoping there was some magic key that would clue in our wives. We wanted them to know our desires without having to express them. We really wanted to avoid a conversation that felt as if we were begging for sex.

Eventually we did talk to our wives, though not when they got to the top of that pass. The conversations were very difficult. For myself, even though I regularly tell people to communicate with their spouses about their sex life, I hate to even bring up the subject with my wife, Karen. I feel awkward asking her when we can have sex or how our sex life is going. Such discussions just feel weird. I'm not sure they will ever feel normal.

Just as difficult as talking to your spouse about sex is two men admitting they do not know how to deal with sexual issues. Greg took a big risk that day. Men seldom have open, honest discussions about their sexual concerns. It doesn't matter whether you're single or married; men don't like talking about their fears and what they perceive are failures. But our discussion opened new avenues in our friendship, which continues to grow deeper.

Another reason this book is needed is that as fathers we don't know how to teach our children about sex. Here again, I've struggled as much as the next guy.

One recent Sunday afternoon Karen and I put our children down for a nap. Then we decided to make love. We felt safe, as the kids usually cooperate for rest time. Just as things were getting hot, however, our six-year-old daughter, Rachael, walked into our bedroom.

Now, being the informed and open parents that we are, how do you suppose we reacted? Why, with total embarrassment, of course. Then Rachael asked what we were doing. "Ah . . . Ah . . . hugging and kissing" was our impressive response.

"How disgusting!" she replied.

How in the world do we talk to our kids about sex? We don't want them to think sex is disgusting; we want them to think marital sex is great. But like talking to our wives about sex, we find this extremely difficult and uncomfortable. We need some guidelines, and this book will help provide them.

FOUNDATIONS

Even more basic than knowing how to talk to our wives and our children is understanding what God created sex to be and how He wants to be involved in that part of our lives. But here again, our understanding is woefully lacking, because Christians do not talk about sex. We don't really want our friends to know about our sexual struggles. We can ask for prayer about financial, spiritual, family, and health issues. But can you imagine a prayer meeting where men requested prayer for "my struggle with masturbation," "my problem with premature ejaculation," or "a better sex life in my marriage"? What a refreshingly honest church service that would be!

God knows we struggle with sex, however—it's no shock to Him. He wants sex to be great in our marriages. He also understands the struggles of the single man. He knows we need His wisdom, and He's willing to work with us. We do not have a God confused by our problems. Yet some believe God would be unsympathetic, even repulsed, by our sexual concerns. But we cannot surprise God, and He certainly won't be offended, if we tell Him the truth about our desires. Our God is a God of grace. He loves us and accepts us where we are. We don't have to earn His love. He is comfortable discussing our sexual issues, and He has provided ways to help us.

One of those ways is through the church and Christian brothers. And in that context, we need to feel the freedom to admit our struggles, to hear that they are normal, and to express our sexuality and our frustrations. But as Jim and I were discussing the title for this book, we realized we would have to title it in such a way that it would be "safe" to buy or borrow. So we decided against titles like *Men Who Struggle with Sex* and *Sexual Males.* Those titles would be difficult to check out at your church library. That's too bad. We hope this book contributes to a more open yet responsible discussion about sex.

LET'S BE HONEST

Yet the thought of risking such a discussion can create a great deal of fear. I remember an experience early in my ministry while leading a group of men and women through the wilderness near Durango, Colorado. These were mature Christian leaders who were the backbone of a ministry. One of the goals of the trip was to develop intimacy. So during one of the discussion times, I opened up about some of my past sexual experiences. What a mistake!

I had thought the group could handle a frank discussion about sexual issues. I was wrong. My ability to be in ministry was instantly called into question. There was no response to my openness. What I received instead was a cold "We will pray for you."

After that experience, why would I again risk sharing my sexual problems with anyone? Because I firmly believe that all men have sexual struggles. There are different levels of struggles, but having sexual doubts and questions is normal. And sharing our struggles in a safe setting, when we can find one, is both freeing and healing.

Today, as I look back at that incident, I realize how innocent I was about people. I had actually set myself up for rejection. But I believe that in the right setting, with trusted friends, we can be honest about our deepest secrets. We all need such Christian friends to help us deal with sexual questions and doubts. Jim and I hope that this book will open up such discussions, in the process improving our friendships, our marriages, and our parenting skills.

In the next two chapters, we'll look at some of the root causes of our sexual frustrations; they are traced to false images and myths stirring in our society and even our churches. Then in chapters 4 through 6, we'll give a biblical perspective to sexuality. In chapters 7 through 12, we'll make that perspective practical in real life. Single men, chapter 8 is devoted entirely to your situation. And in chapters 9 and 10, we'll try to provide understanding help for sexual addiction and some of the common sexual dysfunctions. Throughout the book, we have also included a number of short "Sexual Insights" to give you quick access to topics men often ask us about.

Let's be honest. Let's be practical. And let's allow God to begin the healing process in our sexual lives.

TAKE ACTION

1. On a scale of 1 (terrible) to 10 (great), how do you feel about your sex life? (Circle the most appropriate response.)

   1 2 3 4 5 6 7 8 9 10

   Why?

2. If you're married, how do you think your wife feels about it, using the same scale?

   1 2 3 4 5 6 7 8 9 10

   Why?

3. Have you ever talked to a friend about sex? Do you talk to your wife about sex? What is your greatest fear in talking to a friend or your spouse about sex?

4. What questions do you have about your sexual feelings and experience? Make note of them, and be looking for answers as you read through this book.

2

THE HOLLYWOOD MAN

The "Hollywood Man" is that strong, invincible, always right image of manhood and sexuality that has been popularized by the movies and television. As a popular image, Hollywood Man seems to be everywhere, thanks to the pervasiveness of television and movies in America. If that concept were true to life and you were a Hollywood Man, life would always work. Romance would last forever. Problems would be solved in sixty minutes—two hours tops. Men would cower in your presence. You would be "built," sensual, and able to seduce the most beautiful of women. Sex, which would last for hours, would be the ultimate erotic experience, fireworks exploding into the sky.

The influence of this image can be seen in many popular misconceptions about men and sexuality. To see how much your thinking has been shaped by the Hollywood Man, answer the following true-false questions, read the rest of this chapter, and then check the correct answers at the end of the chapter.

TRUE OR FALSE

1. ________ 50 percent of the married men in the U.S. have had at least one extramarital affair.
2. ________ Men have affairs for sex.
3. ________ Sex comes naturally to men.
4. ________ Men need to have sex to relieve themselves.
5. ________ The divorce rate is 50 percent, showing the weakness of marriage as an institution.
6. ________ Sex outside of marriage is better than marital sex.
7. ________ Fathers rarely teach their sons about sex.
8. ________ Men talk to their wives about their sex lives.

WHO IS THIS HOLLYWOOD MAN?

The Hollywood Man is the man of the movies. He's the man our fathers tried to be and we grew up wanting to be—confident, calm, under control, and unemotional. The Hollywood Man first appeared in all his glory in the sixties with James Bond. Today he is played by men like Clint Eastwood, Michael Douglas, Dustin Hoffman, Tom Cruise, and Arnold Schwarzenegger. He is cool, strong, and able to take on an army of men singlehandedly, but also sensitive, romantic, and incredible with women. Females may try to resist him, but eventually they all give in.

The Hollywood Man is sure of himself with women. He is sexually intelligent, never doubting his ability to please and to perform. He can have intercourse for an hour. And he is never a virgin! He does not struggle with thoughts of homosexuality and never has sexual dysfunctions.

The Hollywood Man is seldom married, however. He believes sex in marriage is boring; the best sex is found outside a long-term, committed relationship. If the Hollywood Man is married, he is having an affair. That may cause some problems, but the sex is worth it. As media critic Michael Medved puts it, "In fact, television treatments of romantic relationships strongly suggest that sensuality is most satisfying when it is shared outside of marriage, and that long-term alliances only serve to diminish the pleasure of the partners."[1]

Success is almost always a given for the Hollywood Man. He's a winner in business, sports, and anything else he chooses to do. He can be tender at the right time, then face death without a tinge of fear.

The life of the Hollywood Man is not mundane or boring but exciting. He is on the edge, rugged, risking life and limb. He does not need support from male friends to make it through life but is comfortable being alone. And, of course, the Hollywood Man never struggles with self-doubt.

The Hollywood Man is the man no one could ever be, yet the very man we think we ought to be.

More specifically regarding sex, the Hollywood Man is convinced that there are women who want sex the Hollywood way—that is, they want sex all the time and are turned on by aggressive men. Numerous films portray sex as a powerful, almost violent act. In the hit movie *Basic Instinct,* for example, sex becomes more powerful because it is dangerous.

During my counseling I have met many men who have begun to think like the Hollywood Man. Listen to their creed:

"Sex is the key to a good marriage." (Bob, a thirty-five-year-old, married ten years)

"Men can't help themselves. They've got to have their sex." (Ted, a twenty-three-year-old single man)

"When I get married, I can have sex anytime I want, and it will be the greatest!" (Rich, a twenty-seven-year-old engaged to be married)

"I always believed that Christians should refrain from premarital sex, but I wanted to be a man too!" (Ken, an eighteen-year-old college student)

"My sex education came from movies, TV, and a joke of a sex education class in junior high." (Rick, a thirty-six-year-old married man with two children)

"I always thought marital sex would be like the movies. Wow, was I wrong!" (Don, a twenty-eight-year-old newlywed)

I (Rick) understand why those men feel that way. I sometimes wish I could be the Hollywood Man. Romantic and passionate sex would be at my fingertips. I would find success in love, career, and with my family.

James Bond was the first Hollywood Man, and perhaps the ultimate one. Beautiful women were always around this debonair secret agent, waiting for a night of romance. If I were Bond, I would never settle down to one woman—too boring. I would not

SEXUAL INSIGHT

EXTRAMARITAL AFFAIRS

As a marriage counselor, I have talked with scores of men who have had sexual affairs. Married men enter into affairs for many reasons. Some have affairs because they have drifted from their wives due to a lack of dealing with conflicts or other problems and an unwillingness to talk about those problems and to deal with them in constructive ways. Some men have affairs to prove to themselves that they are still attractive or to affirm their masculinity. Others are attracted to the conquest.

Still others truly believe they have "fallen in love"; having little feelings toward their wives, each is attracted to a woman who seems to care and possesses qualities that are appealing. And there are some husbands who seek out affairs in order to "pay back" their wives who the men believe have intentionally hurt them.

Dave Carder catalogs three types of affairs in his revealing book, *Torn Asunder* (in chapter 2). The first type is called *the one-night stand*. In this sexual relationship, the man has little emotional connection. He may visit a prostitute, pick up a woman in a bar, or have an unplanned sexual encounter with a friend. There is no pattern of behavior; a one-night stand is just one night.

A man deals with this by admitting the affair and being honest with his wife. The man must show repentance and the wife must grant forgiveness. If this type of affair is not dealt with (talked about, followed by repentance and forgiveness), it can destroy a marriage. In some cases professional help is needed to understand the meaning of the affair and measures to prevent another affair from taking place.

The second type is *the entangled affair*, which develops out of an emotional relationship. These affairs begin as friendships that lead to feelings of love. In the entangled affair sex is not the sole focus; the relationship and love are as important. This type of affair can last from ten days to even ten years, as the man attempts to maintain his marriage.

This type of affair is the most difficult to deal with and will need professional help. The man who truly confronts this affair and dissolves it will undergo a grieving process afterward and a gradual healing process. The marriage will need to undergo a rebuilding process, often as long as the affair has lasted.

Finally, there is *the sexually addicted affair*. Here a husband typically has many affairs over the years, and they all focus on sex. The man finds sex the compelling reason for extramarital involvements. These affairs usually lack strong emotional connections; indeed, men involved in such affairs may have more than one affair occur at the same time or other sexually addictive activities taking place.

Dealing with this type of an affair can be a one- to three-year process for both the husband and wife. These affairs, after all, are addictive in nature. The shame and guilt, the abusive childhood, and the addictive cycle must all be dealt with. (See chapter 9, "Sexual Addiction" for specifics on recovery.)

As we will see in answer 6 of the Self Test (page 30), affairs almost always are unfulfilling and painful, according to researchers Masters and Johnson.

Suggested Reading

David Carder and Duncan Jaenicke, *Torn Asunder* (Chicago: Moody, 1992).

Mark Lasser, *The Secret Sin* (Grand Rapids: Zondervan, 1992).

fear death and could whip ten men by myself. I would have more money than I could spend.

Hollywood Man also appears in TV commercials. In a recent commercial, two men were across the stream from a party of beautiful women (the promised land). As one of the men began to wade in, his buddy saved him from the jaws of an alligator. Oh, no! How in the world would they get to the promised land?

Then one of them opened a bottle of beer, and this "cold draft" froze the river. Thanks to the beer (the savior), the men could walk on water to the promised land of perfect women waiting just for them.

We know that's fantasy and just a commercial, but there is a message. This is life! Women waiting for us. Beer gives us the help we need. "Real men" will overcome problems. We hate to admit it, but most of us wish life was like that.

Now that I'm married and have children, I want life to be like *Home Improvement*, the popular TV show. I want my family to find me incredibly funny and our problems to work out in thirty minutes. I want my wife to be successful and for there to be plenty of money to go around. My marriage should be full of laughter, and our sex life should be fun and easy. Our marriage should also be conflict-free. I wish I had a neighbor like Wilson to talk to about problems, a mentor to help me through life.

Though most of us won't admit it, Hollywood has helped us to often view women as little more than objects of sexual desire. The women in many of the movies I remember were as interested in casual sex as men. I thought women were turned on by the size of a man's muscle, his strength, and even the size of his penis, much the same way that most men are turned on by a woman's physical shape.

Consequently, I thought women would want sex simply for the physical pleasure. I did not think women needed a relationship for sex to be great. Women in the James Bond movies seemed honored to spend one evening with him, even though they'd never see him again. They would turn their backs on their countries just for a night with agent 007.

There is a part of us that believes in the man of TV and the movies, the Hollywood Man. That part would like the powerful romance of Hollywood to be a daily experience. Of course, the Hollywood Man is only one influence on our view of sex. Our overall culture, parents, and friendships also affect our views. The interplay of all these can be seen in Bill's life.

Sexual Freedom

Bill was raised in a family with traditional roles. His dad worked, and his mom stayed at home to rear the children. "My dad never spoke to me about sex. I always saw my dad as a good man and pure in his ways. I did not really understand all that my father had been through. My dad seemed like the perfect man, strong, logical, and moral. I saw him as independent, not needing Mom, and I never pictured them having sex. They just did not seem like sexual people. My dad acted like sex was not important to him and was never a struggle. I saw him come on to Mom once, but she just brushed him off."

Bill's dad served in World War II and actually had several sexual experiences during and after the war. Yet Bill was sexually ignorant. His parents seldom spoke to him about sex. In fact, they seldom spoke of sex to each other.

Bill's father's heroes were men like George Bailey in the movie *It's a Wonderful Life*—community minded, above temptation, strong, and sincere. The idols of the fifties, in contrast to the sexual, sensual idols of the later generations, were almost asexual. Bill's idols came from Hollywood; his father's idols were the local policeman or the hometown baseball hero. Bill's heroes were the rebels his own age; his dad's were older and often examples of morality. And, as part of the consumer-oriented baby boom generation, Bill was influenced to seek more for himself.

"My father did his very best for me by giving me the best money could buy. I believed that I could have it all. I would not have to put myself through college, and if I stayed in college, I would not have to fight in the Vietnam War. I was unique, better and more wise than my own parents."

Bill's heroes were liberated and not bound by the old morals. They could have it all, a free ride and free sex. As one expert observer put it, "The lessons hammered in by parents, teachers, television, rock 'n' roll and the youth culture were taking hold. The people of the boom generation believe that they were something new under the sun; a new generation with a unique sensibility and the power to use it. Theirs was a revelation of rising expectations."[2] Bill expected life to go his way. He could do whatever he wanted, and there was enough money to make life a breeze. Then disaster struck.

When Bill was sixteen, his mom filed for divorce. "This tore me apart," Bill said. "I never could talk to my dad about the divorce. This experience left me feeling lonely and isolated. In my friendships, I had no clue how to talk to them about my pain. We spent a great deal of our time watching movies. The Hollywood Man came into my life promising pleasure and true masculinity. I found myself dreaming of being James Bond, independent, unreachable, above emotional issues and smooth with women."

Bill also felt betrayed by his parents. "When I was growing up, my parents acted like they had it together. They never had problems, at least none that I ever saw. Then one day, bam, it's over. They are no longer married, no reason given, no conversation about what happened. Their whole marriage felt like a lie. I just stopped believing anything they stood for."

He could see his parents' hypocrisy and the materialism in their generation. He got the message that to grow up would corrupt you. He did not want to become like them. Bill also began to see his parents' stuffiness regarding sexuality. He rejected those values too. He wanted to be part of the Woodstock mentality, whose sexual openness was at least honest.

THE RESULT

As Bill continued to grow, his discussions with other boys centered on girls and how far they had gone with them. Bill desired to be accepted. But he was confused inside. Girls seemed like a place where he could find love. Bill recalled, "I had hoped that a girl would be able to understand my struggles, but I found it very difficult to trust a female with my heart. During this time, girls became more like objects than human beings. Love became simplified; love was sex. I began to have sexual relations in high school. My buddies thought I was pretty macho."

This pattern of behavior continued into college, where Bill was in one relationship after another. He thought he was living a liberated life. He had cast off his parents' morality for a freedom in "love." He expected to stay young, like his Hollywood heroes. He rejected materialism, competition, the work ethic, sexual taboos, and laws regarding drugs and patriotism. Yet in rejecting the establishment, he still expected that life would go his way, that he would not struggle financially, morally, or emotionally.

"I wanted to experience true intimacy, but I felt unable to work through simple problems in my relationships. True intimacy during this time in my life was equal to sexual freedom. Eventually, I got one of my girlfriends pregnant. I was scared, but I acted as if it didn't phase me. I paid for her abortion. Man, I was totally confused. The concept of free love didn't apply in this situation. Free love produced a baby, and now I was paying to have that baby removed so I would not have to face the responsibility of my choices. I had believed that life would just go my way. Part of me wanted a real relationship, but during this time I did not know who I was. I kept hoping that sex and good times would bring me happiness."

Instead, Bill remembers, "I was more lonely and in more pain because of my sex life. I did not love this woman; I didn't really know her, for that matter. I did not even know myself."

A New View of Sexuality

During this perplexing period, Bill began meeting with a fellow student who had a deep relationship with Christ. "This guy had gone through the Jesus movement during the sixties," Bill says. "My friend was not only a strong Christian, but also a real person. He did not pretend he didn't struggle with some of these same issues; he was open about his own pain."

Eventually, Bill believed the Christian message. Then he started understanding how different Christ is compared to the Hollywood Man. He had taken for granted that men need to be sexually involved to be "real men," but now he began to see that a healthy view of male sexuality involves the whole person. He realized that men need intimacy with God, women, and friends. He learned that a loving marriage means more than good sex—that sex should be part of a deep, committed relationship, not something to be bought.

All this is not to say, however, that Bill's struggles regarding sexuality disappeared overnight. He continued to fight the Hollywood Man, trying to transform his mind.

Today Bill is married and has three children. As we sit over coffee and breakfast, we talk about life and the Hollywood Man. Bill reports, "Now I can see through the Hollywood Man. I realize that life is not like the movies. I work at my marriage, I work at loving my children, and I enjoy learning how to follow God. To be honest with you, I still sometimes wish life was like Hollywood.

. . . [But I remind myself that] life is not about great sex; life is about great relationships."

GREAT EXPECTATIONS

Both his father and the Hollywood Man had a deep impact on Bill's life. In the case of Russ, the impact of his father shaped him more than the images from Hollywood, but the Hollywood myth also played a role in how he viewed his sexuality.

On the outside, Russ's childhood family looked perfect, like the Cleavers in *Leave It to Beaver.* On the inside, it was cold. To Russ, this was normal. The way his family kept up the image was to avoid problems, and it seemed to work.

"I thought I grew up in the perfect home until I got married," Russ says. "All of a sudden, I realized I did not know how to communicate. I was cut off from my feelings. I wanted things to just work out.

"I realized the lack of emotional connection in my parents' relationship created the model I was beginning to live out. My father had been trained by our culture to unplug himself from his feelings. This created a disconnection between my father and me. This disconnection aided in my ability to disconnect sex from relationship."

Russ did not talk with his dad about love, marriage, or, especially, sex. Bernie Zilbergeld points out the danger in that situation and also points to a partial answer:

> Boys in such situations often don't get what they need. After being admonished hundreds of times to be strong, to shape up, to stop acting like a sissy, boys learn to hide their feelings and to act tough regardless of how they feel. The result is adult males who are always pretending to be someone they're not and who are fearful of letting anyone know what's going on inside.
>
> Little boys, like little girls, like to touch, hug, and kiss, but parents, especially fathers, stop touching their boys early. Although affectionate touching is a general problem in our culture, especially for males, something needs to be done about it if we want our children to be better prepared for intimate relationships than we were. . . . Despite all the sexual titillation, our culture is one of the most touch-deprived in the world, and our males are the most touch-deprived people in it."[3]

Like so many fathers, Russ's dad worked long hours away from home, spending little time with Russ. This set up a situation where Russ's mom did all the child care and his dad felt left out. In the home, it appeared that Mom was in charge and Dad was responsible only for discipline. Without a strong connection to his dad, Russ was left on his own to find out what being male is all about.

He soon bought the Hollywood Man myth. "I spent more time with the Hollywood Man than I did with my own father," Russ says. Once he accepted the Hollywoood myth of masculinity, his heroes became James Bond and Rambo. "Watching TV and movies helped me believe that sex is something a 'real man' gets. My dad and I never really discussed sex, so I figured he agreed with the Hollywood Man."

Russ became sexually aggressive, only to find much disappointment. "I tried several times to initiate sex, only to be turned down. A couple of more rejections caused me to doubt my masculinity. I would tell my buddies I was not a virgin just to save face. I had no males to turn to except the Hollywood Man, who never discussed the struggles of being a man. I continued to doubt my masculinity throughout college. I would sit around and talk with my friends about how great sex was, never knowing many of them were virgins too.

"I felt like the weirdo. I was not sexually involved but felt I would be happier if I were. I wanted to experience sex without the emotional entanglements. I believed sex in marriage would be boring. I thought commitment would mess up your sex life."

Says social critic Christopher Lasch, "Exclusive attachments gave way to an easygoing promiscuity as the normal pattern of sexual relations. . . . The most prevalent form of escape from emotional complexity is promiscuity: the attempt to achieve a strict separation between sex and feeling. Here again, escape masquerades as liberation, regression as progress."[4]

For Russ, sex became a value in and of itself. The focus of sex was pleasure, not relationship. He believed the promise of the Hollywood Man that great sex can happen without emotional connection. When Russ finally married, however, he found this promise unfulfilled.

"My wife would turn me down if we were having problems," Russ says. "I found myself expecting marital sex to be like the movies. I thought something was wrong with me when I would achieve orgasm only minutes into intercourse. I dreamed of being able to have sex for hours and my wife screaming with delight."

A further dilemma was that while Russ wanted to be a man committed to his marriage, he doubted his masculinity because he was not sexually experienced.

BECOMING A MAN IN THE NINETIES

In the nineties, the Hollywood Man is a mixture of roles. Men are supposed to be as tough as Arnold Schwarzenegger, as sensitive as Kevin Costner, and as smooth with women as Richard Gere.

Sex continues to be a major focus of movies and television. As Michael Medved says,

> The erotic references on network television are neither as intense nor as omnipresent as those in popular music, but to a surprising extent they convey the same underlying message: that sex should be viewed as an end in itself, a glorious form of recreation that has nothing to do with responsibility or commitment.[5]

Consequently, many men who desire to be committed to one woman often feel they are strange and maybe not as masculine as the playboy types.

Pre-teen and adolescent boys of the nineties are being raised on MTV, where music videos show them that women want sex. Many of the videos denigrate women. There is not even a question of the rightness of premarital sex. And on an episode of *Married with Children*, a TV show popular with teens, the parents are worried because their son can't get sex.

The Hollywood Man is still giving sex education classes daily, and his message is crystal clear: Sex is great anywhere, anytime, with anyone. To believe differently is to be weird.

THE EXTREME OF OBSESSION

What kind of person is today's Hollywood Man producing? The obsession with sexual experiences can lead to men like Curt. He's an eighteen-year-old sex addict hooked on pornography and masturbation. As he sits on my office couch, he tells me his story: "At age eleven, I found my father's pornographic magazines. I soon found myself with an erection and learned how to masturbate. By the age of twelve, I was masturbating one or two times a day. The shame and guilt led me down a road to depression."

"I wasn't able to form good male friendships. I thought people could tell I was obsessed with sex. I didn't date much in high school. I was intimidated by girls. I became more and more lonely and secretive."

Curt's isolation and obsession with his secret made it difficult to concentrate at school, and soon he concluded his habit was incurable and his life "hopeless. I believed my family would be better off without me. One evening, I took a bottle of pain relievers and laid down to die. I was so depressed and lonely that I could see no reason to stay alive."

His parents found him and rushed him to the hospital. Two weeks later, he ended up in my office.

Does Curt's case sound extreme to you? I am sad to say that many young men in our culture are growing up like Curt, believing that sex will solve their problems.

The Effects of the Hollywood Man

The Hollywood Man continues to push men toward an obsession with sex, which can create a multitude of problems. What is an obsession with sex? It's sex on the brain, where life revolves around thoughts, actions, and feelings about sex. Sex is seen as an end in itself. We want sex to relieve stress and to feel loved. We focus on technique, and sex becomes a measure of our masculinity unrelated to commitment. Sex that is not risky or dirty can't be great.

Those are some generalities. Let's look specifically now at some of the ways the Hollywood Man affects different aspects of our lives.

Marriage

In our marriages, we set ourselves up for problems because of unrealistic expectations and feelings of failure. We think our wives are indifferent or even frigid in their sexual responses and that we deserve more and different sex. We expect good sex to come naturally and therefore believe we don't need education and practice. We believe the misleading statistic (see page 30) that one of two couples divorce each year and that half of all married men have affairs. And, of course, because TV and the movies never show a married couple working through a sexual problem and finding fulfillment, we don't know how to do it and aren't even sure it can be done.

Singleness

For many single men, sex is their cure for loneliness and a relief from their pain. Sex can become the primary way they show love. Just being single and not sexual creates struggles with masculinity. The pressures of society and specifically the popular arts (embodied in the Hollywood Man) make single men wonder whether they should remain celibate. In fact, some feel there is a defect in their personality if they're not sexually active.

Friendships

In our friendships with men, we end up feeling isolated or fearing closeness. We certainly fear being honest about ourselves and our sex lives. We avoid real intimacy with a friend to evade feelings of normal affection.

View of God

When we accept the Hollywood Man as our model, God becomes the ultimate killjoy, the old man who is angry because we feel sexual. We begin to believe He is out of date and does not understand our modern world. God grows distant and is unavailable for help. The Hollywood Man encourages us to grow self-sufficient, needing and having only our own strength to meet our needs. Hollywood Man has us believing our faith is a weakness, that we are uptight and without a clue about how to really enjoy life.

Families

We feel insecure about our role as men in our children's lives. We try to be this tough Hollywood type and grow emotionally distant from our kids. We shy away from discussing sexual issues with them. We feel we don't live up to the ideal of a "real man" in the area of sexuality and success. The Hollywood Man whispers in our ears, "You fail too much, and you doubt yourself too much. But whatever you do, don't show your kids that life gets to you, that you don't have all the answers."

In short, the Hollywood Man is a cultural myth that encourages us to think that sex is our greatest need and that the right kind of sex will take away our pain and make us complete. It leads to totally unrealistic expectations of ourselves and of marriage, as well as to damaging practices. Believing in the Hollywood Man is a setup for pain, loneliness, unfulfilling relationships, and misdirection in life.

GRADING YOUR SELF-TEST

How did you do on the true-false quiz at the beginning of the chapter? Perhaps in reading this chapter you have revised some of your opinions; certainly the acceptance of most of these statements shows us the amazing influence of the Hollywood Man on our views of sex. As you will see, all the statements except one are false.

1. *At least 50 percent of the men in the U.S. have had an affair.*
   False. The news media seem to indicate this, but a recent study by the University of Chicago's National Opinion Research Center found that four of every five married men in the U.S. are faithful to their wives. Only 21 percent have ever had an affair, and at the time of the study, only 5 percent had been involved in an affair in the preceding twelve months. Including married women, the study found only 15 percent of spouses are unfaithful in marriage.[6] This follows a 1987 ABC News/*Washington Post* poll that found only 11 percent of spouses unfaithful.[7]

2. *Men have affairs for sex.*
   False. The majority of men who have affairs do so because of an emotional involvement. (Men who struggle with sexual addiction, however, do sometimes have affairs simply for the sex.) Men who succumb to extramarital affairs typically are looking for love, acceptance, and respect. A man can be attracted to another woman when such feelings seem missing in his own marriage and seemingly being offered on the outside.[8]

3. *Sex comes naturally to men.*
   False. Sex is a learning process. Good sex develops through communication and a committed relationship. Most men

limit their communication, either because of poor modeling and training by their fathers, or a fear of being vulnerable as they show they have needs. And they are unsure how to please a woman sexually, having bought many of the "instant response" myths of the Hollywood Man.

4. *Men need to have sex to relieve themselves.*
False. Men do not need to have sex to relieve pressure. The male body will either reabsorb semen or release it through nocturnal emission (wet dreams). A man can say no to his sexual urges as surely as he can say no to drugs or an excess of food.

5. *The divorce rate is 50 percent, showing the weakness of marriage as an institution.*
False. The divorce rate is actually closer to 25 percent. The common figure of 50 percent is spread by "illogical mathematics and the unthinking acceptance of this 'fact' by scholars, journalists, politicians, and public figures," says George Barna, a researcher in California. Barna says the confusion arises from combining data from two sets of people. In any one year, the people who get divorced and who marry "are, for the most part, different people. It is not possible to claim that half of all marriages end in divorce simply because this year we had two times as many people get married as got divorced."[9]

6. *Sex outside of marriage is better than marital sex.*
False. A Masters and Johnson report on human sexuality published in 1986 has found that men involved in affairs considered marital sex more satisfying.[10]

7. *Fathers rarely teach their sons about sex.*
True. Only 10 percent of American males were told about sex by their fathers.[11]

8. *Men talk to their wives about their sex lives.*
False. Because of fears about their masculinity and uncertainty about how to broach the subject, men do not talk about their sexual concerns and desires to their wives, much less talk about sexual issues to their sons. The men I counsel with find sex a difficult subject to discuss and seldom talk about it outside of initiating it.

TAKE ACTION

1. Who were some of your TV and movie heroes as a boy?

2. What did their exploits teach you about what it means to be a man? How did they treat women? Did they ever seem confused or fearful about sex?

3. Name a recent movie or TV program you've seen that contained a message about male sexuality and masculinity. What was the real message about men?

   Now think about how this message might affect your view of yourself and your sex life. Do you measure up to the message?

4. Write a paragraph to a ten-year-old boy about how he should handle and interpret today's popular media.

3

THE CHURCH MAN

What in the world is a "Church Man"? In chapter 2, which discussed the Hollywood Man, we saw how our modern, popular culture creates unrealistic expectations that tend to produce an obsession with sex. In a similar way, the Church Man also has a set of impossible expectations. Specifically, the Church Man is a person who was reared in the church and has adopted a view of his sexuality that's often reflected in repressed sexuality or "stuffed" sexual feelings.

Don't misunderstand. We're not antichurch. However, the church has a powerful ability to influence and instruct people, not only about values and morals, but also in terms of how they view themselves. Therefore, the church has a responsibility to help men understand clearly what biblical sexuality is about. And far too often, it fails in that responsibility. To show what we mean, let's meet Mike, a typical Church Man.

Mike's Story

"I grew up in the church," Mike says. "My parents were Christians, and I accepted Christ as my Savior at a young age." As a professional in his mid-thirties, he has been around the church enough to "know all the biblical answers." He knows all about right and wrong, and he is quite active in his church.

Through the years, Mike has become a master at "impression management." That is, he manages to look just like what those around him expect. This is a useful skill in business as well as in the church. "I wouldn't dream of talking about sex in church," he says, although he may occasionally hint at having sexual feelings. After all, knowing what to do with your sexual feelings is part of being a Church Man. Any time he does discuss sex, which isn't often, it is with other males he knows outside the church.

Mike admits, "I have flirted with pornography. I've 'checked out' and read *Playboy* and *Penthouse*. I've watched a few X-rated videos and even visited a topless bar."

He states this without pride nor regret but only as a matter of fact. For him, such actions may be wrong, but feeding his sexual urges seems acceptable, part of being male. In his entire life within the church, Mike has received essentially no instruction about sexuality other than hearing sermons about the evils of immorality. "What I learned about sex while growing up came primarily from friends, usually older friends." Very limited instruction was provided by his parents. "I came away from the one-time sex talk with my father with the idea that sex is dirty, but that I should save it for the one I would come to love. Figure that out!" This confusing message contributed to his confused feelings about sex.

Thus, Mike's understanding of manliness and sexual things came mostly from the culture. And though the church correctly told him that the culture misrepresents sex, the church never provided him with a better education.

Mike has never had a sexual affair. That's not to say he hasn't had the opportunity, however, because Mike is handsome, clever, and definitely attracts the ladies. He has been married sixteen years and at times has lusted after other women. He considers his attraction to women as proof positive of his depravity and sinfulness.

The church has strongly reinforced his self-condemnation and helped him to feel even more guilty about his sexuality and humanity. The grace of God, which made his salvation so real in other areas, has failed to apply to the sexual side of his nature. So he lives in constant tension that he must find some way to alleviate —some way to handle—those sexual urges that cause him to feel guilt and shame.

To do so, Mike began to develop ways to avoid and escape from his feelings and problems. Psychologists refer to this way of coping as the use of defense mechanisms. As he grew up in the church and faced his adolescent sexual feelings, he was filled with tension and frustration. He experimented with where the line was between right and wrong, and although he did not go "all the way" (sexual intercourse) with any of his dates, he did go to a point just short of that. Since he had not technically lost his virginity, he believed he was doing OK. As one trying to imitate the Church Man, in this aspect he felt good about his behavior.

"In some cases, I was even the one who had to tell the girl no," he says, which increased his pride in his "virginity" but did nothing to ease his sexual frustration. This is a contrast to the Hollywood Man, who takes pride in losing his virginity.

Mike experienced intercourse for the first time with his wife-to-be before marriage, and this "doomed me to marrying her," he says with a trace of bitterness, "especially since we were now already married in God's eyes." Marriage was the first real outlet for his sexual urges, and sex was satisfying for a while. However, since no biblical foundation for a healthy relationship had been laid, his restlessness grew, and his needs for sexual fulfillment were not met.

Mike found he had difficulty being completely honest with his spouse. In fact, that kind of vulnerability frightened him. "I was sure that if she knew the 'real' Mike, she would reject me." But by not taking that risk, he began to experience feelings of rejection from her anyway. This increased his feelings of anger and frustration toward his wife. Gradually their sexual relationship began to change, and they had sex less often. Mike spent less time at home, becoming more involved in his work and in other activities such as athletics. Ironically, he even increased his involvement at church.

Mike wondered whether masturbation was sinful, but he still practiced it regularly as a way to get some satisfaction. "Sex with myself seemed safer than sex with my wife," he says, "and it required less effort." He began to convince himself that he didn't need to have sex to be happy and that it was just the pressures of society that made sex so interesting and tempting. While Mike knew all was not well, he didn't talk about his sexual feelings with anyone lest his church friends see him as being something less than spiritual. To anyone watching him, he appeared to be happily married.

SEXUAL INSIGHT

LUST

Biblical prophets and modern-day preachers rightly warn us against lust, which when indulged results in "adultery" in our hearts (Matthew 5:28). But what is lust and how do we control it?

Because we are sexual beings, some of our thoughts and images will be sexual in nature. Unless you have totally stuffed your sexual feelings, you will have to cope with sexual thoughts and be aware when a light fantasy moves into sinful lust.

Fantasy becomes lust when a person wants to possess another or makes a plan to make the fantasy happen. Casual feelings of attraction to another person do not qualify as lust, yet left unchecked they can lead to an obsession where one wants to act on his feelings. This is lust.

Lust begins in the mind and happens out of our natural selfish desires. Lust occurs when we begin to make someone or something so important that it becomes a god unto itself. Lust is perverted love. For while love is honoring and giving, lust is for taking and getting at the expense of others.

We learn to address lust by taking charge of our thought life (2 Corinthians 10:5). Here are five suggestions:

1. Confess all evil thinking as sin (1 John 1:9).
2. Recognize that lust as a sin is appealing and addictive.
3. Acknowledge the real price of lust in terms of your time, energy, and impact on your relationships.
4. Stop feeding lust. Whenever possible, avoid suggestive material, such as pornographic magazines, and many movies and TV shows.
5. Build fantasies on what God would desire for you. God wishes us to strive for purity. Guide your fantasies about the woman you may marry: how you will treat her, how you can prepare for marriage. Or if you believe you are not called to marriage, dream of future vacations where you can enjoy God's creation and perhaps deepen or develop a friend's spiritual thirst. If married, focus on the love and beautiful qualities of your wife.

Sexual intimacy is altogether good in marriage. In sexual relations we are giving pleasure and uniting in spirit and body. In lust, whether married or single, we are exploiting the other person. Lust, in fact, is an act of running away and avoiding intimacy. Therefore sexual desire is good and God-given; lust is selfish and part of our sinful nature (Colossians 3:5).

Suggested Reading

Richard Foster, *Money, Sex, and Power* (San Francisco: Harper & Row, 1985).

Edwin Louis Cole, *Communication, Sex and Money* (Tulsa: Harrison, 1987).

Mike began to gain weight as he turned to food as a form of self-nurturance, a way to help him feel better about himself. When he couldn't stand the extra weight he'd gained, he would become obsessed with an exercise program.

"I realized I was becoming a lonely man," he says sadly. That was true because he had not developed positive and healthy communication with his wife. It was difficult for him to express his frustration and the anger he felt from not having a healthy sexual relationship. "I wondered if my wife was having sex with me only out of a sense of duty, which felt far less satisfying than if it were a mutual desire." In the meantime, he received attention from other women, and they became the objects of his masturbatory fantasies and lustful longings. He did, of course, feel guilty about these things, but "I figured that if I didn't try to have an affair, I hadn't really 'crossed the line.'"

It seemed to Mike that his church ranked its sins, with sexual sins being by far the worst, so Mike looked for excitement in other things, and he convinced himself that the arousal in these activities was not so bad because it didn't involve sex. At his job he found excitement in his work, getting compliments for a job well done and feeling good in completing a challenging project. Sometimes he engaged in quick flirtations with female coworkers. During leisure time, he escaped into athletic involvement and watching sports on TV; and at one time he dabbled with gambling to be stimulated.

Mike, like all of us, was looking for approval and acceptance. He often sought ways in which he could experience positive strokes by pleasing people and doing things well. Since he did not feel good about himself and he didn't experience acceptance from his spouse, he was determined to find approval and acceptance elsewhere.

Mike had the biblical head knowledge of what it means to be intimate in the marital bond, but he had never experienced it personally. After years in an unsatisfactory relationship, he began to believe it was not possible in his reality.

Hollywood Man Vs. Church Man

The Hollywood Man and our culture encourage and teach sexual license and unrestrained freedom. The church, on the other hand, often teaches a set of strict rules governing how we are to deal with our sexuality. Unfortunately, many times the law the church teaches isn't necessarily consistent with the law that Scripture encourages, especially with regard to the liberty we receive in Christ.

As a result, men feel restricted and have an incomplete and limited view of their sexuality. It doesn't help for us to move toward license, of course, but neither does it help for us to move strictly toward the law side. Rather, the challenge is to discover how liberty fits into an understanding of sexuality and to see that the Bible deals with the boundaries of sexuality somewhere between law and license.

The focus on sex in American culture can make sex a god unto itself. Indeed, the Hollywood Man makes an idol of sex by defining our sexuality as entirely genital, and with this comes impossible expectations. But we can also make an idol of sexuality when we treat it as a taboo with the power to hurt us if we become too familiar with it.[1] Again, this is what often occurs in the Church Man. In other words, sex has the power of a demon, so it should be avoided and not be too familiar to us. The contrast here is between the impossible expectations of the culture and what feels like the impossible expectation of the church, which is to not feel sexual at all.

We need a healthy balance and boundaries that come from a more accurate understanding of Scripture. Without it, both the Church Man and the Hollywood Man share the same trap—they make the phallic symbol into a god. We might say that culture assumes that sex is genital and therefore good, whereas the church has accepted the cultural view that sex is genital and has concluded that sex is therefore evil.

In both cases, a problem exists because the cultural view of sex is accepted as the truth about a man's sexuality. We will see in chapters 5 and 6 that sexuality is much, much more than just an aspect of one's anatomy.

Is Sex Negative?

Whereas the Hollywood Man seems to leave a man feeling inadequate because no one can measure up to the Hollywood image, the Church Man results in a person feeling guilty or inadequate spiritually. One of the problems inherent in traditional Christianity is how the church gives people this negative attitude toward their sexuality.

This chapter is called "The Church Man" because it focuses on how men who grow up in conservative, evangelical churches often do not receive any significant sexual education or healthy and positive understanding of their sexuality. Their education instead has taken place elsewhere in society, in schools, locker rooms, magazines, TV and the movies. What results is a man who is tremendously confused. Many men believe that having sexual feelings is to be unspiritual, and often separate their sexuality from their Christianity, as if the two exist in separate worlds.

This antisexual tradition in Christianity did not simply appear in the twentieth century. Negative attitudes toward male sexuality have probably been around as long as Christianity itself. One beginning may have been the early Greek or gnostic idea that the spirit is good and the flesh is something bad.[2] This became a particular problem in the Corinthian church, where people believed, "That's not me, it's just my body. If my spirit is redeemed and is good, that is what communes with God. If my body or my flesh is depraved, it doesn't really matter what I do with it." There was some question about whether a person could even control the flesh, so men surrendered to it, resulting in considerable sexual immorality.

One early church leader, Augustine, saw the struggle against evil as a call to struggle against sexuality. He could not imagine an innocent person in Eden would have sexual desire. In other words, "A sinless Adam could never have been turned on sexually by a pure Eve."[3]

Another early church leader, Origen, was so intent on ridding himself of sexual desires that he castrated himself. This may have been a too literal interpretation of Matthew 5:29–30, which refers to cutting out your offending eye or cutting off your offending hand. This type of thinking encouraged virginity and emphasized celibacy, so that by the fourth century, the church ultimately made a decision requiring celibacy for the priesthood (though the decision was far from unanimous).[4]

The orthodox position on marriage swung back and forth through the centuries, with one camp viewing it as a "blessing from God," while the other viewed it as a "necessary evil." By the time of the Protestant Reformation, a number of reformers rejected the notion of a celibate clergy and believed that married sex was one of God's good creations. Calvin wrote, "Conjugal intercourse is a thing that is pure, honorable, and holy because it is a pure institution of God." This teaching ignited a considerable debate between the reformers and the Catholic Church, which ultimately charged the Puritan theology and the Protestants with "sensual and licentious living."[5] So we see that the church's negative attitude toward sexual desire and expression has been around for quite some time, and Christian men often have felt guilty about their sexual feelings.

Learning to "Stuff" Our Feelings

How do our views on sex and Christianity affect the way we relate to our wives (and girlfriends if we are single) and to other men and women who are important to us? Why do we have all these ways to hide and protect ourselves from getting hurt? What prevents us from experiencing a healthy sexual or intimate relationship?

Most people don't know where to begin. What they see is the secular view, the Hollywood Man image. They are told clearly in their churches that this position is wrong, even bad. The alternative view, which is not presented clearly in most churches, is the biblical view, that of intimate sexuality. We are told superficially what we might expect, but in terms of applying it to our lives, we are given no clear examples of how it's to happen. Like Mike, we come to the conclusion that it is not possible in *our* reality.

A typical result is that men and women, to avoid becoming sexually obsessed, become sexually repressed. In many churches, this system of sexual repression is actually reinforced and prized. Both boys and girls receive little sexual information that is helpful and healthy. Think about your own church. Now, or as a child, does or did your church encourage you to feel positive about yourself as a male? Do you receive teaching and direction in Sunday school? From the pulpit? Or is sexual instruction such a "hot potato" that it is ignored and avoided?

Of course, the Church Man is not alone in using hiding strategies. The Hollywood Man also has problems with being open and honest. It isn't just Church Men who run away from intimacy. Hollywood Men act the same way, following culture's example. Unfortunately, imitating the Church Man has the same result —not because of what Scripture says, but because the church encourages men to act a certain way. Often the church and the men want to portray a certain image, one of pleasing others. As church men we have learned to please people and look to others for a sense of identity instead of looking to Christ.

One reason the Church Man is popular in our churches is that we men aren't good at drawing close to other men and helping each other understand how to be open and honest about our feelings. Nor do we help each other identify our forms of avoidance and escape.

The Antidote to the Church Man

The Church Man thrives; the church is not effectively helping men fully understand our sexual identity. Our churches need to be offering responsible sex education rather than always promoting a negative point of view. The primary antidote to the Church Man is the Biblical Man, who understands and expresses his sexuality according to the biblical model. (He is described in depth in chapter 5.) A second way to remove the influence of the Church Man is for the church to offer accurate, helpful sex education that begins during our children's formative years.

If the church were teaching sex education, sexuality and spirituality could develop together, which would, in turn, foster healthy marriages. Too often, however, boys become men who associate sex with something fun and exciting outside marriage and outside the church; then an adrenalin rush of guilt adds intense passion to sinful sex. But teaching that sexuality is a God-given force within us, a power that can be used either positively or negatively, helps people make wise decisions. We will either hide our children in an environment based on fear, or we will protect them by giving them the facts with which they can make good, value-based decisions.[6]

For example, the goodness of our bodies and of our sexual natures can be taught in Sunday school as early as kindergarten. Since kids are exposed to it, handling "dirty" language and the importance of "good touch" can also be addressed. In prepuberty, explanations of sex and what makes it right or wrong can begin to expose children to God's purpose for the family and marriage. Adolescence is the time for frank dialogue regarding dating, dealing with romance and sexual attraction, and developing moral discernment about petting. It also is an opportunity to make a clear case for chastity and ongoing character development.[7]

Sex education doesn't have to stop with the kids either. Adult education should include classes on how to develop intimacy and communication. Clarifying and implementing sexual values is important whether one is single or married. Learning to foster healthy, intimate relationships with other men, women, and children is essential if we're to overcome the Hollywood Man and Church Man mentalities and begin producing authentic men of God.

Sex is a powerful, important aspect of our lives. It creates such intense emotions that people like Church Man, in an effort to control them, have developed a variety of ways to push them out of mind. These hiding strategies can take so many different forms that in the next chapter, we will explore some of the more common ones that become roadblocks to intimacy.

TAKE ACTION

1. If you "grew up in the church," what kind of sexual instruction did you receive while growing up?

2. How comfortable are you with discussing sexual issues with male friends in your church? Do you have a close Christian friend with whom you can talk about this subject? If not, think about some Christian acquaintance with whom you might be able to risk a discussion about sexuality. You might begin by asking him about his sexual education in the past and how the church affected his understanding of sex. You might also talk about why it seems so difficult to discuss this subject without embarassment.

3. To what extent and in what ways does your church communicate information about sexuality?

4. In light of what you've read so far, how might your church improve its efforts to teach a healthy view of sexuality?

4

MEN IN HIDING

As human beings, we were created to be in relationship with one another, to be close to each other. Sexual feelings are part of that drive for closeness. However, the message of the church often has been "Watch out, sin lurks there!" As a result, we often associate sexual feelings with trouble; so we find ways to avoid the trouble—to avoid sex or any feelings associated with it. When we avoid our natural, God-given sexual feelings, however, we run the risk of avoiding closeness with our spouses, our friends, and our children.

People have dozens of ways to avoid their feelings and thus closeness. Those techniques are what psychologists call *defense mechanisms* and what we will refer to as *hiding strategies.* They can be employed by anyone.

We also use those strategies because we're afraid of rejection, and they limit our ability to draw close to another, even a spouse. Hiding strategies may be defined as "habitual and unconscious techniques used to reduce or avoid anxiety or the awareness of something unpleasant. They help us to deny or distort the real sources of anxiety and maintain an idealized self-image so that we can live with ourselves."[1]

Hiding strategies are almost always, to some extent, self-deceptive. They deny, falsify, or distort reality. They are ways in which we lie to ourselves and often others.

Generally speaking, however, when feelings or urges are stuffed or repressed, especially sexual feelings, they have a way of leaking out in some manner. This is one reason to deal with them head on. Beyond that, God intends for us to face our problems, to move through struggles in order to become stronger, "mature and complete, not lacking anything," as it says in James 1. He promises us in Philippians 4:13 that we "can do all things through Christ who strengthens." So let's look honestly at ten hiding strategies men commonly use.

1. Repression

George was in his early forties and had been married for nearly twenty years. He and his wife, Helen, had enjoyed a reasonably active sex life, but then something occurred to change that. George's mother-in-law came for a "brief" visit. However, she injured herself while there, and the brief visit turned into a six-month stay.

Helen felt it was important to try to help restore her mother to health, and she devoted much of her time, energy, and attention to that task. On the surface, George agreed this was the kind and Christian thing to do. But then things began to change in George and Helen's sex life. Their lovemaking occurred far less often and with considerably less enjoyment.

George began to feel as if he really didn't want to have sex with Helen at all. He was normally a kind and generous man, but now, in public, he began to make sarcastic jokes and comments regarding his mother-in-law. He found himself becoming increasingly negative about many things in life and marriage.

"I knew I had no right to be angry. After all, we were doing the reasonable thing to care for my mother-in-law. But I have to admit that I was feeling increasingly hostile toward both my mother-in-law and my wife." Initially, though, George was unaware of his extreme anger. Eventually through counseling he recognized and admitted those feelings, and he also discovered how fearful he was that his mother-in-law would change his relationship with Helen.

As George and Helen began to deal with those fears and feelings in counseling, his sexual desire for her began to increase again. His sarcasm began to decrease. His normal optimism and positive attitude returned.

George's sexual desire had been inhibited by repression. That is, he "stuffed" his thoughts and feelings about a subject without being aware of what he was doing. His repressed feelings and thoughts toward his wife and mother-in-law continued to influence his personality.

Repression of our sexual feelings has several consequences. For most men, including George, the result is inhibited sexual desire. George didn't seem to care about or need sex, but he was actually angry at his partner.

A second consequence may be sarcasm. In sarcasm, we deal with our anger through humor and thinly veiled hostility, which can easily hurt people. As one wise person said, "It takes a smart husband to have the last word and not use it." George expressed pessimism or negativity, which voiced a concern not only that his mother-in-law was present, but also that she might never leave and his relationship with his wife might not get back to normal.

George also admitted that he was afraid to express his feelings because he didn't believe they were justified. He was concerned too that stating them might increase the conflict with his wife.

The hiding strategy of sexual repression works like this: You're angry with your partner. You may have been hurt. You may feel burned. But you don't want to face the discussion and the work required to resolve the differences, so you repress those feelings and avoid the person sexually. In a sense the issue is "out of sight," or at least out of your awareness, but it is not out of your mind. And if you don't face your sexual feelings, the internal frustration can make you angry. What sets you off can be anything, and it might have nothing to do with sex. You might be angry at your mother, your boss, the garbage man, the kids, and so forth.

2. Somatization

Henry, in his late twenties, recently married a woman named Diane, who had been married previously and had a history of being promiscuous. Henry had been celibate. Although he loved Diane very much, he worried whether he would be able to please her sexually. She was interested in developing a committed relationship with Henry and had long since been forgiven for her past indiscretions.

Diane had a strong sex drive and looked forward to a healthy, positive sex life with Henry. As a result, it was not unusual for her to initiate sexual relations. Henry was not completely aware of the degree of anxiety he was experiencing, but whenever Diane began to snuggle or cuddle with him, he found himself developing a headache. At times, he responded to her advances with heartburn or diarrhea. At one point, he experienced chest pains and was sure he was having a heart attack. This was later discovered to be a panic attack.

Henry was using somatization as his strategy to hide from closeness. He was very anxious, and he was convinced he would not be able to measure up to Diane's expectations of him sexually. After all, she was far more experienced. This anxiety leaked out in physical ways.

In somatization, hiding our emotion creates a real physical problem. Approximately 80 percent of the population uses some form of somatization regularly.[2] We may feel angry at our wife or someone else close to us, but we don't become aware of it and may experience a headache as a result. We may feel frustration and, as a result, have heartburn or diarrhea. Such a physical problem can appear far more acceptable than admitting an emotional or sexual problem.

This hiding strategy extends far beyond the sexual arena. At work, we may develop physical symptoms after the boss begins pressuring us; the physical response allows us to withdraw. Even at church a person may feel ill after someone asks him to teach a Sunday school class. Somatization is an involuntary response that can occur whenever a situation creates a threat of vulnerability or embarrassment. Though somatization may involve stress —a "perceived threat or demand"—it includes the hiding of a particular emotion (such as anger or anxiety) and the developing of a physical condition that allows us to withdraw.

For Henry, the emotions were anxiety about Diane's expectations. During counseling with Diane, he expressed those feelings of anxiety; as their communication improved, Henry and Diane were able to resolve the problem in healthy ways.

3. Rationalization and Intellectualization

Rationalization is a fancy word for making excuses. The making of excuses comes from a natural tendency to explain our behavior. The explanations are often rational, reasonable, and convincing—but not the real reasons. Thus we say a person is rationalizing. In rationalization, a man will offer some plausible excuse for his sinful behavior. It's another way of using your head to try to distance yourself from any feelings.

In the case of the Church Man, he may rationalize that he has to work or be involved with his church duties, so he can't spend time with his wife or children. In fact, he doesn't want to deal with a sexual issue and thus hides the problem through another explanation. Mike, our example of a Church Man, rationalized that the sins and obsessions he used to create arousal were not so bad because they did not involve sex, which he believed to be a worse sin.

Closely related to rationalization is intellectualization. In this strategy, we remove or isolate emotion from a situation by talking about it formally and intellectually, or at a distance.[3] We become clinical and detached, and in so doing, we try to avoid feeling possible consequences. Sometimes we succeed, becoming almost robots, untrue to our actual feelings.

I (Jim) catch myself utilizing intellectualization when I don't talk in feeling words to describe relational issues I am facing. When I use big words, it can serve to further distance me from my feelings.

There are two consequences of denying our feelings. First, we are dishonest, at least with others and often with ourselves. We hinder effective communication as we analyze our behaviors and attitudes without feeling them. Second, when we intellectualize, we ignore a part of who we are. We become all head and little heart, and our heart of feelings and passion is part of our very being. God wants His commandments not to be written just on tablets of stone, but also on the heart. When we keep it in our head, we miss out on the blessings God has for us.

4. Denial

Charlie was in his late thirties, with a successful career as a banker. He worked hard and was a good provider. Two children were in high school when his wife decided to take a job outside the home.

June was an attractive woman, and Charlie was proud she was his wife. She enjoyed her new job and began to purchase clothes to update her wardrobe. Her skirts became shorter, her hairstyle changed, and she began wearing a different perfume.

She told Charlie of a co-worker who was quite helpful to her in her new job. In fact, this male co-worker had offered to spend additional time to help "show her the ropes."

June was gradually gone more and more from home, and she and Charlie spent less and less time together. When a friend told Charlie that he had seen June at a restaurant with another man, Charlie thought nothing of it because he knew his wife was doing business. When another friend mentioned, with some concern, that he had seen June and another man come out of a hotel room in a neighboring community, Charlie again stated that he trusted his wife and the person must have been mistaken.

When June came to Charlie a few weeks later and said she wanted a divorce because she had fallen in love with someone else, Charlie could not believe it. He was shocked. She had to be kidding.

Charlie was practicing the hiding strategy of denial. *Denial* means to protect oneself from an unpleasant reality by refusing to accept it.[4] Charlie was blind to what became obvious indications that June was having an affair. Had Charlie recognized and addressed the warning signs as he and June drifted apart, he may have prevented the developing affair and prompted work on their problems.

Later, when June's affair broke off, she and Charlie went for counseling. Interestingly, she then told Charlie that she had hoped he would notice some of the changes she was making and express concern and a willingness to fight for her.

"When you didn't, well, I guess I let myself be attracted to someone who was showing me much more attention."

June also became more obvious in her acting out, hoping Charlie would "wake up and smell the coffee." Yet Charlie had refused to believe his wife would have an affair. He didn't want to believe he needed to do more work on their relationship. He tried to pretend the problem was not there instead of facing it, dealing with the conflict, and attempting to understand what was creating the separation.

"I thought it was easier to not deal with it; that seemed the way to avoid any pain if she actually were involved," Charlie told me. "I guess I didn't want the conflict and the effort it would take to resolve any problems between my wife and me."

Denial is powerful in creating an illusion that is more palatable than reality. It often involves some naïveté, a situation Proverbs 14:15 and 16:2 address. In self-deception we tell ourselves, "If I deny the feelings long enough they may go away. If I deny them long enough, I may not have to deal with them." When we deny our sexual feelings or fears, we delude ourselves into thinking they do not matter. Though we refuse to acknowledge a problem, it still exists. Eventually those sexual desires will reappear and be as strong as ever.

If we are not careful, we can either shut down those desires —not be able to feel sexual feelings with our spouse—or find them expressing themselves in some distorted way—homosexuality or fetishes, for example. We are created with an innate sexual appetite. It is not OK to become anorexic with regard to our sexual feelings.[5] We have to cope with them in some way. To promote the illusion that they are not there results in a roadblock to intimacy.

5. PHARISEEISM

Phariseeism is one of the most common ways a Church Man can avoid dealing with his sexual feelings or being honest with himself or others. In phariseeism, a person develops self-righteousness or appears to be self-righteous to avoid looking at himself. He may be engaged in the practice secretly, while publicly he criticizes it.

Jesus' parable of the Pharisee and the tax collector in Luke 18:9–14 illustrates this point. The Pharisee was proud that he was not like others, and thus he exalted himself. The tax collector, on the other hand, acknowledged his sin before God and was humble. Jesus said that the humble man went home justified and that the one who exalted himself would be humbled.

The modern Pharisee convinces himself of some inherent goodness to cover his sins. What results is a hypocrisy in our churches in which people appear to be holy and spiritual on Sunday morning but are far from it in their daily practice and relationships.

Hypocritical self-righteousness is an attempt to protect ourselves from the truth about our sense of inadequacy in trying to measure up to Scripture or the standards placed on us by others.

We all struggle with sex and sexual sins either occasionally or all the time. To claim that you never do may mean you're hiding behind phariseeism.

6. Control

Scott is the head of his home. In fact, if you don't do things his way in his home, you will be in big trouble. Scott regularly quotes Scripture to his wife regarding her body as being his and under his control. She has sex when Scott wants it. When she protests, she is told she is evil and out of God's will. Scott believed that whatever he wanted was God's will for his wife.

When someone tries to assume control or actually exerts control over another person, he is often reacting to a sense of inner powerlessness. He attempts to control someone or a situation so he isn't left with that sense of helplessness or forced to deal with feelings that seem to be out of control. And often it's the sexual feelings that can lead a person to feel out of control. The idea is this: "If I control my environment, my situation, or the people around me enough, perhaps I will then be able to gain some control over the sexual feelings."

7. Fantasy

Dick loved to daydream, and his favorite fantasies involved sex. He had an OK sex life, but it could never measure up to his daydreams. In his fantasy world, he was an awesome stud. When things got difficult with his wife, Dick went to fantasyland quickly. She could be talking on and on, but while he looked attentive, he was really somewhere else.

In Dick's fantasy, he was always right, always the best, and always ready to perform. Not surprisingly, when Dick had sex with his wife, he was only using her body, because in his mind he was making love to the new girl at the office, or the woman on the video he had rented the night before.

Sexual fantasies are not unusual. A person can develop a fairly extensive fantasy life in which he can lose himself in a world that is more acceptable and enjoyable than the real one.

In one study, researchers found that students attending a lecture spent nearly one-fourth of the class time daydreaming about sex.[6] In fantasy, frustrated or unacceptable needs and motives may be freely expressed. Daydream topics can indicate which of a person's needs are being frustrated.

Fantasies don't have to be bad. In fact, daydreams have been called the "nursery of great achievement." Fantasies can help define future plans and aspirations as one tries on various roles and lifestyles. However, fantasies become a problem when they are used too often as an escape from reality.[7]

In Dick's case, fantasy became a problem because it was his way of withdrawing from his wife. He'd rather do anything than have to focus on a relationship he didn't like or have to deal with the fact that he had sexual feelings with no acceptable outlets.

8. Passive Aggressive / Passive Dependent

Eric was a nice guy. He was helpful and kind to everyone but his wife, Jackie. She was pretty, talented, bright, and opinionated. She was also a hard worker and an effective leader. Eric could recognize and acknowledge most of those traits, but to him, she was also demanding, intimidating, and impossible to please. Jackie loved affection. She craved closeness and honest communication. She even enjoyed sex.

Eric was never openly nasty or verbally abusive. He never yelled. Remember, he was a nice guy. But he was angry at Jackie and would not admit it. Instead, his anger came out in a variety of other ways. He procrastinated in tasks she wanted done. She liked neatness, and he was messy. He lied to her regarding insignificant details.

One of the most hurtful ways Eric displayed his anger was sexually. He wasn't rough or demanding. In fact, it was usually up to Jackie to initiate sex. What he did instead was to ejaculate within a few seconds of entering her and then roll over and go to sleep. Eric also chose not to become very erect for his wife.

Eric was using passive-aggressiveness as his hiding strategy and as a way to display his anger. He didn't openly express his anger; instead he "got even" indirectly.

Passivity can be a major roadblock to intimacy. It may take the form of being a "wimpy man," or it may be displayed as uninvolvement with or indifference toward one's spouse. Indifference is the opposite of being truly loving. Remember that a man using a hiding strategy is often angry under the surface because he is not getting his needs met.

Passivity may be teamed with aggressiveness. As with Eric, this is not overt aggressiveness. Instead, it takes less direct forms like stubbornness, procrastinating, pouting, or always being late. The person may be purposefully inefficient or use sabotage. If any suggestions to improve the relationship are made, he finds ways to show why they won't work. Another classic passive-aggressive tendency is the use of drugs or alcohol.

9. PROJECTION

Ed was a jealous man. According to him, his wife was an incredible flirt. He had to keep his eye on her because she was so easily attracted to other men. Although he couldn't prove it, he was sure his wife had been unfaithful.

Ed was amazing at placing blame. In fact, nothing was ever his fault. When I saw him and his wife in counseling, however, it was because of his affair. His wife had not been unfaithful, but he used his belief that she had to justify his own adultery. Friends of Ed's, especially women, would tell you that Ed was a remarkable flirt. But that was something he could not admit or see in himself.

Projection is the hiding strategy Ed illustrates. A person who is projecting, or blaming, unconsciously transfers his own shortcomings or unacceptable impulses to others. By exaggerating those unacceptable traits in others, the individual lessens his own failings.[8]

Perhaps the most common example of projection is an experience everyone has had. Some days, everyone you meet seems friendly and in a good mood, while on other days, everyone seems unfriendly and unhappy. What's happening is you are probably projecting what you feel to those around you. The chances of everyone you meet being in a good or bad mood simultaneously are rather slim. Obviously, the strong feeling is in you.

When a man is using projection, he says, for example, "You lust after me" instead of the unbearable truth "I lust after you." Men can become especially proficient at this in their marriages. As someone once said, "When it comes to broken marriages, most husbands will split the blame—half his wife's fault, and half her mother's."

10. SUBLIMATION

A final hiding strategy involves the use of sublimation. In this case, a man puts his focus on something else to avoid dealing with whatever is the threat. When his sexual feelings seem to threaten him, he will find substitute behaviors to protect him from dealing with his sexual desires.

Remember our Church Man, Mike, at the beginning of the last chapter? He became a workaholic to avoid facing the stressful relationship with his wife. He also turned to food to avoid facing his sexual desires and as a way to nurture himself. He followed that by sublimating his sexual energy into exercise, which generally is a positive outlet but for Mike became another way to hide from his wife.

With sublimation, a person can turn to other "affairs" that may not be sexual in nature, such as work, hobbies, or even TV watching. Sublimation is getting our arousal and acting out the sexual frustration in other ways. Sometimes those other ways are compulsive in nature, but since they may not be perceived as being as destructive as sexual compulsivity, we convince ourselves that they are acceptable.

Hiding Strategies and Intimacy

Everyone uses hiding strategies, and they all serve to block closeness. In Genesis, we have the example of Adam and Eve and how, in their prefallen state in the garden, they were naked and unashamed. There was no hiding. There was no blame. They were able to relate to one another openly and experience healthy intimacy. When guilt and fear were introduced as a function of their sin, there arose a need for clothing and hiding, and they were ashamed.

In many churches, sex equals sin on many occasions, and thus shame and guilt become associated with that. Somehow we miss the notion of grace and liberty that comes with being Christians who are able to function in God's image.

In the next chapter, we will look at what the Bible teaches about sexuality so that we can begin to gain an understanding of healthy relationships and how to develop them. The first step, however, involves finding the courage to be honest with ourselves. Will we be candid enough to admit how we lie to and deceive ourselves? The irony of hiding strategies is that they only need to be effective enough to fool the person using them. It becomes irrelevant whether other people are also fooled.

In the children's story "The Emperor's New Clothes," the emperor was convinced that he had on absolutely beautiful clothing, but the truth was that he was naked, and everyone was afraid to tell him he was playing the fool. Hiding strategies are much like the emperor's clothing. We think we've got something special going to protect us, but we become the fools as we rob ourselves of the opportunity for authentic expressions of our sexuality.

TAKE ACTION

1. Try to think back and identify your earliest sexual memories. These are the images that first revealed your maleness. They may have occurred in toilet training, semi-sexual play with other children, changing in the school locker room with other boys, or perhaps even being exploited sexually by someone. Do these images evoke positive or negative feelings? Do they cause you to feel strong and valuable or anxious and shameful?

   What thoughts and feelings do you have in response to this exercise? Our strategies for hiding are learned early in life. If you have had mainly negative feelings toward your sexuality, you have had years to practice and perfect those strategies and to learn new ways of hiding. Though we are not responsible for how we were reared, we are responsible for what we do about it.

2. Which of the hiding strategies discussed in this chapter have you used to protect yourself from getting close? Think about how you developed the strategy and who in your life now tends to "benefit" from it the most. Remember, hiding strategies are generally forms of self-deceit. We have to be very honest with ourselves to even recognize that we are using them.

3. After thinking about Take Action 1 and 2, take a few moments to express to God what you have discovered about yourself. Praise Him for positive memories and images, or tell Him about the hurt and shame. After all, God has complete knowledge of all that you've experienced. His love for you is unconditional (Psalm 31: 7, 16). Discuss with Him the hiding strategies you recognize and the ones you use. Ask God for help to be honest with yourself and others.

5

THE BIBLICAL MAN

One day, the Creator and His Son were discussing the week they'd had. The Creator said, "Let's make a man."

"A what?" the Son responded.

"We've been busy this week," said the Creator, "and we've put a lot of interesting creatures on this little planet. Let's make a man to take care of it. Let's make a man who will have the ability to appreciate it. He will be the culmination of our efforts."

"What will this man look like?" inquired the Son.

"We'll make him like us—at least in our image. That way, he'll be able to recognize us, respond to us, talk to us."

Spirit, who was overhearing this conversation, said, "Will you give him choice?"

"Now, what would the completion of our creation be without choice?"

"I'm sure you know what that means," said the Spirit.

"Of course, if he has the right to choose, he'll make good decisions and bad ones. He'll please us and disappoint us. But what's a relationship without choice? He'll be able to get to know us and come to understand who we are. And with his mind, he'll also be able to understand and appreciate what we've made. I realize that in giving man choice, We risk making life exciting, if not chaotic. Believe me, we'll all have an important part to play in the drama that will begin. So let's get busy."

Then the Creator reached down into His garden, scooped up some dirt, and molded it in His hands. He breathed into it, and man was born. The dust became a living being with flesh and blood, thoughts and emotions, and an ability to make his own choices.

We now will take a close look at the creation narrative found in Genesis 1–3. By looking at the first man and woman we find clues about our own sexuality. We also learn what a Biblical Man is. There are plenty of clues as the story continues.

The Creator commanded, "Adam, wake up!" As Adam opened his eyes, the first thing he saw was his Creator. The Creator smiled, and Adam smiled back.

The Creator was fully satisfied with His effort and laughed as He said, "This is good! This is very good!" And His joy and laughter filled the universe.

Adam looked at his hands and feet. He began to look around him. It was beautiful. It was paradise. His senses were taking it all in, and he felt strong. He also felt safe and secure. It was good.

The Creator put His arm around Adam's shoulder and began to walk him around the garden. He talked to him about what He wanted him to do; he was to care for the garden. The Creator also gave him the job of naming all the other creatures. He wanted Adam to enjoy himself and enjoy the creation. Most of all, He wanted Adam to enjoy the Creator and get to know Him. Adam had a good understanding of what the Creator wanted, and he gladly chose to do it.

Adam was a "real" man, the prototype, and was perfect from the start. As he looked around the garden, he noticed that the other creatures were paired with another version of themselves. They seemed to come in various complementary forms. Each was as beautiful as the other. But Adam saw that he was alone. He had no complement. Everything in his world was perfect, yet it seemed incomplete.

One day, as he walked with the Creator in the garden, he asked the Creator, "See those lions over there?"

The Creator smiled and answered, "Yes."

"I named them 'lions,' of course. But one seems a little different than the other."

"The one with the hairy mane is a male, and the one with him is a female."

"What's a female?" Adam asked.

The Creator laughed again and said, "I wondered when you'd get around to that. Adam, you're perfect. But you lack another part that will make you complete. I just wanted a chance to get to know you first and let you get to know Me before We made you a partner.

"See, Adam," the Creator continued, "it's not good for man to be alone. I will make a helper suited just for you. You've learned an important lesson, Adam. You've learned the importance of being close. Our relationship has already taught you that. It's taught you to yearn for and crave closeness. This has helped you draw closer to your Creator. It has also taught you that there is a missing piece you need to be complete. Another human being. I want you to take a little nap; I've got some work to do."

Adam laid down, and the Creator began a fresh, impressive creation. He opened Adam up and selected a rib right next to Adam's heart. He gently broke it off and removed it from Adam's body. With one smooth move of His hand, He closed Adam's chest, and he was healed. He took the rib and breathed on it, fashioning an incredibly beautiful creature. Then He nudged Adam awake.

"Man, I have a surprise for you!" He told Adam. "I'd like to introduce you to someone very special, for I've saved the best for last. I'd like you to meet Eve."

Adam opened his eyes and could not believe what he saw. Out of his mouth came the word *woman*, for he knew this creation had come out of him and was like him, yet somehow different.

Adam was awestruck. His senses were blasted the first time he saw the Creator's handiwork, but this time he was overwhelmed. He felt at once excited and fulfilled. He was satisfied.

Adam slowly got to his feet and walked over to the woman.

He reached out and touched her. Her skin was like his. He began to explore her with his hands, and she responded. He pulled her close to him and held her. They looked into each other's eyes and seemingly into each other's souls. If ever there was love at first sight, this was it. She smiled. Again, the Creator was pleased, and as He laughed, you could feel the heavens rejoicing.

SEXUAL INSIGHT

GOD AND SEX

As designed by the Creator, our sexuality is part of being made in God's image. The Church Man often believes "The less sexual I am, the more spiritual I can become." But this is a myth. Our sexuality is part of our identity.

Here are several truths about God's purposes for and attitudes toward our sexuality:

- God is the creator of sex, and He was pleased with all that He made. God also understands sex and your sexual feelings.
- God gave us our sex drives not to make us miserable but to bring us fulfillment in relationships. Enjoyment of sex in marriage is appropriate. The sexual act is not just for making babies but is also intended for pleasure between a husband and wife. It is a blessing from God.
- God intended sexual intimacy for the committed relationship of marriage. God created us as sexual creatures with sexual drives and feelings.
- God intended sex to be intimate communication. Sexual touching is a process of communication that uses the body to express love from the spirit, emotion, mind, and will.
- God desires that sex be a celebration of our relationship. When our relationships with our spouses are healthy, sex will be great. If problems exist in the marital relationship, sex will suffer accordingly.
- God created us as sexual beings to instruct us about Himself and the purpose of our sexuality—that we were created to be in relationship and that we are incomplete in ourselves and need others to experience completeness.
- God also uses our sexual identities in marriage to illustrate the value of self-giving and of sacrificial love. Sexual expression is the most satisfying when we give pleasure to another person.
- God provided the sexual union in marriage for couples to experience complete closeness, to be united, to be "one flesh."

Keep in mind that sexual union in marriage is more than becoming "one flesh." As Bill Hybels notes in *Tender Love,* physical oneness "is designed to be the culmination and consuming expression of a relationship that is growing in love. Only when a man and wife relate at the level of heart and mind, in a trust-filled, open, safe, vulnerable, loving, passionate kind of way, does sexual intercourse represent what it was meant to represent: ultimate unity. Take-your-breath-away intimacy."

Suggested Reading

Lewis B. Smedes, *Sex for Christians* (Grand Rapids, Mich.: Eerdmans, 1976).

Clifford and Joyce Penner, *The Gift of Sex* (Waco, Tex.: Word, 1981).

As Adam looked upon her body, he noticed she was different from him. But he liked the difference. She was rounded in some areas and scooped in others. Everything about her was meant to complement him, to satisfy him. Let's face it, she was the perfect woman. It was good. His arm seemed to fit right around her shoulders, and her arm seemed to fit right around his waist.

Adam began to walk her around the garden and show her all the Creator had made. He showed her the jobs he had to do. He gave her the names of the animals he'd come up with. This beautiful place was the ultimate antidote to civilization, better than any Club Med vacation. This was paradise.

That evening, as they nestled down together and stared at the stars in the heavens, they held each other in their arms. Adam had experienced other beautiful moonlit nights, but this night was different, better than all the rest. Adam noticed that as he touched Eve's body, it responded to his, and his responded to hers. Adam discovered passion, and as he loved Eve, he began to discover what it felt like to be completely united and joined with his partner. He felt he was becoming one flesh. He felt his body become part of hers and hers part of his. He whispered to himself with a chuckle, "What will the Creator think of next? This is great. I think I'll call this action *sex*, and sex is great!"

Adam and Eve worked together. They played together. There didn't seem to be much difference between work and play—both were enjoyable. Adam and Eve knew each other completely. Emotionally, physically, and spiritually, they were on the same page. They were made for each other. They shared their bodies and souls with each other. They celebrated their relationship with the best sex imaginable. Nothing interfered with their relationship with one another or with the Creator.

Trouble in Paradise

But as surely as there is tension, rivalry and misunderstanding today between the sexes, the tranquility between the first couple would not last. God had given man choice, and both Adam and Eve were about to make a terrible choice that would divide them from God and put obstacles in their relationship. Something happened one day that began to change all that had been wonderful, beautiful, and perfect.

Eve met the snake. The snake had his own story to tell. He'd had his falling out with the Creator long ago. He was determined to try to get even. The snake was good at something Eve had not encountered before. As the "father of lies," he misrepresented the truth. He was deceit in its purest form. Eve had never experienced this kind of communication. Her relationship with Adam was honest and open. They always told the truth; they didn't know anything other to do.

The snake, however, was about to introduce the myth of materialism—that more is better. The snake invented selfishness. He was about to convince Eve that it was good for her. And so he conned her into believing that somehow, splitting off from Adam and the Creator and being her own person was a good thing. The snake deceived her into thinking about her needs, not Adam's. Until then, Adam had focused on her needs, and she had naturally responded to meet his.

But now, Eve grabbed and ate the fruit, and the course of history was eternally changed. Eve had learned selfishness, and it didn't take long for Adam to learn it as well, as he chose to partake of the fruit. The perfect love they had experienced in giving to the other was changed as a result of two bites of forbidden fruit.

Almost immediately, they looked at each other and felt guilty, scared, and vulnerable. They had stepped out of the perfect protection of their relationship with God and sought their own way. Whereas before they had always given to one another, now came this overwhelming sense that the other may be taking instead of giving. And, as a result, there was created the possibility of being hurt by the other.

The First Coverup

That evening, Adam felt like having sex—not making love, but having sex. He didn't like feeling guilty and vulnerable, so he thought a little escape into pleasure might be a good remedy. The two joined together, but somehow this time the oneness didn't feel the same. Oh, Adam had his orgasm, and it seemed as if he may have pleased Eve, but Eve felt used. Adam was rougher than he usually was. He was more insistent.

Just as they'd finished, who should they hear but the Creator coming toward them. Now, not only did they feel distant from one another instead of that one-flesh feeling, but they also felt they needed to hide from the Creator. They had never felt that before. They felt shy and defenseless—and dirty. The Creator entered the garden and began to look for them, which is what the Creator does very well. He constantly seeks us and always finds us.

The Creator called, "Adam, Eve, where are you?" Of course, He already knew. Besides, Adam and Eve were new at hiding and weren't very good at it. And although they would get more practiced at hiding from one another, they would never get good enough to hide from Him.

Before long, the Creator had them found. They had covered themselves with hastily sewn leaves and branches.

"What's the matter?" he asked.

"We're naked," stammered Adam.

The sewing job Adam and Eve had done wasn't very good. It didn't cover them very well; but they would get better at covering themselves. They would get better at escaping and running away. They would run to sex, and they would run from sex. They would run to others, and they would run from one another. They would also run from the Creator.

The Creator, however, fixed them up with some new clothes made out of animal skins. But to do so, He had to shed blood. This had not happened before, but it would happen again. There would have to be more sacrifices. He then sent them out of the garden. He did that for their own good, because if they would have eaten of another tree, they would have lived forever in their sinful state.

When He went back to heaven, the Creator told His Son, "Now it's Your time to get ready. They will need to learn from You about how to get back into relationship again."

That's my (Jim's) version of the true story of creation of man and woman, based largely on Genesis 1:26–3:24. I tell the story at such length to drive home two points. First, we were created in God's image in order to experience relationship with Him. Second, He created us male and female, two aspects of humanity that only find their completeness in relationship with one another. We were made to experience communion and closeness with God and with one another.

God, the Source of Our Sexuality

To understand sexuality, we need to understand our uniqueness as persons and how that uniqueness contributes to intimacy in relationships. God gave us our sexuality. For men, that means our maleness and the drives we possess. Unfortunately, as a result of sin's entering the world, our sexuality and our understanding of women have been perverted.

A prime example of that is how society has come to see sexuality as synonymous with sexual activity—specifically, intercourse. But sexuality is much more. It's a gift from God, part of His perfect order. It's what allows us to experience ourselves as men and women to experience themselves as women. We hope to show that sexuality and spirituality do not represent opposite ends of a spectrum, but that they overlap and are more alike than opposite. This will be explored further in chapter 6.

Sexuality is a drive within us for completeness, for oneness, for wholeness. Thus, sexual behavior becomes a reflection of our understanding of who we are as sexual people. If our focus is on our genitals, and that becomes the god that we worship, we will engage in whatever behavior is necessary to pay homage to it. If our god becomes reflected in laws and regulations, we will do whatever is necessary to fulfill the requirements and experience some degree of satisfaction. Neither of these gods, however, reflects the one true God, the Creator.

No Shame, No Blame

"The man and his wife were both naked, and they felt no shame" (Genesis 2:25). In the Garden of Eden, sex must have been fabulous because the physical bond between Adam and Eve reflected their perfect love. There was no shame and no guilt. Sex was not only for procreation, but also for enjoyment. Adam and Eve were not only naked physically, but they were also naked emotionally and spiritually. There was no hiding. There was no blame. Imagine sex with your mate without any history of sin, with total honesty, no hiding strategies, no sickness or disease, in an environment that was paradise.

This honest relationship continued until sin entered the world. Sin then interrupted the intimacy between God and man and between man and woman. When guilt and fear were introduced, there arose the need for clothing and hiding, and they were ashamed.

Celebrate Your Relationship

The theme of giving up one's own desire and pleasure for the good of the other is repeated throughout Scripture. It is not just sex for sex's sake; it is not just sex for the sake of orgasm; rather, sexual intercourse is intended to be a celebration of the relationship. When the relationship is spiritually and relationally healed, when there is deep communication and trust, sex is going to be better. If there is something to celebrate, sex will be good. On the other hand, when there are conflicts and unresolved problems in the relationship, sex will suffer.

Nor does sexuality stop in the bedroom. The attitude of giving love we should have for our spouses, God also commands us to carry on with others—not so that we can make sex objects out of them, not so that we can exploit them, but so that we can experience an intimacy that comes from fellowship. And as men who learn to give in sacrificial love, we understand our own identities, and thus our sexuality, better. As uniquely different people, men and women can experience an intimacy by having fellowship man to man and man to woman.

There is no doubt that sex can mess up relationships, and that will happen when we are self-centered or narcissistic in our thinking and try to exploit or control the other. But through self-giving, we become more whole as persons. This willingness to serve the other is emphasized throughout Scripture. In Acts 20:35, Jesus told us that it is more blessed to give than to receive. Hebrews 10:24 continues the theme: "Consider how we may spur one another on to love and good deeds."

Scripture speaks of how honesty is foundational to closeness and intimacy. The apostle John writes, "If we walk in the light as He is in the light, we have fellowship with one another, and the blood of Jesus, His Son, purifies us from all sin" (1 John 1:7). Honesty is mandatory for us to be able to address the self-deceit of our hiding strategies. It's also necessary for us to be able to face life's inevitable pain and discuss the uncomfortable so that we can move through the pain, experience closeness, and become more mature and complete (James 1:2–4).

In addition, we are commanded to speak the truth in love (Ephesians 4:15). In fact, the love passages are found throughout Scripture (for instance, John 13:34, 1 Corinthians 13, and Jude 21). Why? Because God intends for us to affirm one another, build one another up, encourage one another, and bear one another's burdens. When we demonstrate those things one to another, we are reflections of Christ. We are also the most effective witnesses it's possible to be.

An interesting progression begins to happen as we start to trust one another and become honest with each another. We then start to become vulnerable with one another, more open to hurt. None of us likes to be hurt, but that vulnerability will lead to an experience of transparency and increased openness. And when we don't experience rejection but instead feel an acceptance, caring, and compassion, we are then moved to a deeper and deeper intimacy. This is a true reflection of our sexuality, not our sexual behavior but our ability to become the kind of people God intended us to be—intimate, close, authentic individuals.

To see this kind of healthy sexuality in the flesh, we need look no further than the example of Jesus Christ. He was a sexual being, a whole person, and apparently single. Let's see how He lived out this part of His humanity.

THE BIBLICAL MANHOOD OF JESUS

Jesus used His maleness and His humanity to relate to other men, to women, and to children. We don't often think of Jesus as a sexual person, but He certainly was not asexual. He was not just God on earth. He was fully human and experienced all forms of temptation (Hebrews 4:15). We can assume that as such, He experienced sexual urges; yet He did not sin. He was sexual, single, and celibate.

Man to Man

Simon was a fisherman, a man's man. He was strong and rugged. Yet something was missing. As he was working on his nets one day, his brother Andrew came up and said, "You've got to come with me! We've found the Messiah!"

"What are you talking about?" Simon said. "People have been looking for Him for years. What makes you think you've found Him?"

Andrew always got excited about things that later turned out to be different from what he'd thought. So Simon decided that maybe he'd better go check this out, just to protect Andrew.

As they walked along, Andrew kept telling him things that had happened and what John the Baptist had said. According to Andrew, John had even called this guy "the Lamb of God." Evidently John and his followers had spent an entire day with this man and had been absolutely amazed at what He had said and done. *Whatever, He must be a pretty great rabbi, teacher, or something.* Simon was definitely curious.

When they reached the clearing where this man was teaching, He looked up, and Simon caught His eye. *Whoa!* Simon thought. *This Jesus can see right through me into my very soul.* Simon was not prepared for what happened next.

Jesus looked at him as He said, "You are Simon, son of John; you will be called Peter."

Peter could not figure this guy's angle. Where was He coming from? *Peter* meant "the Rock." That certainly got him thinking. He'd had some successes before, but Simon had meant "sinking sand." Perhaps he'd better investigate this man further.

Peter did check out Jesus, and as he got to know Him, he began to trust Him. He had never felt loved like this before. Someone had confidence in him and believed in him even when He knew all his weaknesses. Peter was the kind of guy who would open his mouth now and wonder why later. He was the kind of guy who would step right out into a situation (like out of a boat) and later wonder if he should have. But Peter knew Jesus would be there for him. He knew Jesus wasn't going to let him down or let him drown. In spite of the myth that says men don't need anyone or any help, Jesus was teaching Peter that he needed Him. Some things just can't be done alone.

Peter came to understand more and more who Jesus was. Jesus talked about the sacrifice of Himself, about serving others—about things that men just don't do.

Just as God had a plan when Adam and Eve sinned, so Christ had a solution when Peter sinned by lying and renouncing his relationship to Jesus. Not only did Christ die and then rise from the grave, but He also came back to Peter and gave him an opportunity to be restored. Peter thought he'd blown it so badly that Christ would never talk to him again. But Jesus forgave him and still loved him. Even more importantly, Jesus helped Peter feel loved. He was not only Peter's Lord, but He was also Peter's friend. Jesus taught Peter that it was OK to love another man, that loving was part of being a man.

What can we learn from Jesus about our relationships with other men? Jesus demonstrated that in a truly loving and deep relationship, you could mess up and be forgiven, challenge and not be rejected. Peter himself learned the importance of being accountable to another man too. Jesus called on Peter to "Feed my sheep" (John 21:15–19), and Peter welcomed this project. Theirs was a man-to-man relationship in which you could struggle together and talk about things that were important.

Jesus also teaches us about commitment and developing an eternal perspective. Peter responded by committing his life in the name of his friend. As Jesus gladly gave up His life for a friend (John 15:13), so Peter showed his love by doing the same.

Man to Woman

Because we men are influenced by our culture, we tend to see women as sexual objects. Here again, Jesus is our example of a healthier masculinity.

As we read through Scripture, it's interesting to note that Jesus didn't just associate with "Polly PureHeart." In fact, He associated with some women who most of us would lust after. As we will see, Jesus displayed respect and compassion in his dealings with women.

When Jesus encountered the Samaritan woman one day at Jacob's well (John 4), He faced a woman who had reason for many Jewish men to scorn her. Not only was she a Samaritan, which was a big strike against her in the eyes of a Jew, but she had also been "around the block a few times." She would have given Liz Taylor a run for her money in terms of number of marriages. This was a woman with a bad reputation. Perhaps she was an outcast without any friends. One thing we do know is that in a society in which it was frowned upon, this woman had sex and apparently had it a lot.

When she came to the well to draw water, Jesus was waiting for her and asked her for a drink. Now, talking to this Samaritan woman was like a triple play in rule breaking. It was forbidden for a Jewish man to talk to a woman on the street, let alone a Samaritan woman, let alone a bad woman.

When she questioned His request, Jesus immediately started talking about a gift of God, living water, and so on. He recognized her thirsty soul that she had tried to satisfy in a number of ways, most of which were wrong. Jesus then made her aware that He knew all her ugly history and reputation, but He did not use it to embarrass or condemn her. Rather, He used it to help her see that she needed what He had to give.

He also divulged something important and personal to her, that He was the Messiah. He gave her vital details about Himself.

And He did all this and neither tried to seduce her nor was seduced. Instead, he concentrated on her need, as great as that of any person. He recognized she was sinful. She recognized He loved her, understood her, and was forgiving. She received Him as her Savior.

The purpose of His contact with this woman was to see her cleansed, restored, made whole, and freed from guilt and shame. He was not out to use her. Instead, He offered her love, respect, and a new beginning.

Another woman with whom Christ had contact is found in John 8. This woman was "caught in adultery"—apparently right in the act. The focus of the Pharisees who caught her was on meting out justice, on seeing this woman as disgusting and dirty. She was a sexual object to be used or tossed away. Jesus' response was that the person without sin should start the judgment process. Christ, the only one there qualified to do so, did not condemn her but encouraged her to go and have a new beginning, leaving behind her life of sin. He offered her affirmation, support, and understanding. He was able to view her as a beautiful person because he recognized she was created by God. And although she might fail again and again, she was free to live differently.

Interestingly, in many cases it was people who had been burned by sex, who had committed sexual sins, who were so attracted to Christ. And Christ did not reject them or turn them away. They were aware of their need for wholeness and their need to be clean. They were seeking an honest relationship, true intimacy, and they found it in Christ. Jesus neither exploited nor condemned these women, the reactions that could be expected with the Hollywood Man or the Church Man.

Jesus allowed Himself to be loved by others, including women of all types of reputations. He was able to see women as God made them, in need of relationship with God and others. He saw their need to be honored and respected. He knew they valued deep and honest communication and desired an intimacy that would require transparency and vulnerability.

Man to Child

My children love bedtime stories, and one night several months ago one of my sons was having difficulty sleeping. I (Jim) began to tell him stories and would have him close his eyes and imagine the scenes I was painting. By using our imagination, we can go through all kinds of adventures. One of his favorites was the time we went and visited Jesus.

In the story, we were walking through a meadow together when we came upon a clearing. Jesus was sitting on the ground there, with children all around Him.

"It's a beautiful day," I told my son Cole. "The sky is blue, the sun is bright, the air is clean and crisp, and the flowers are blooming." In our imaginative story, animals were scampering around. In fact, a deer came up to Jesus, and He calmly petted its nose. A bunny rabbit with its soft, fluffy tail hopped by, and beautiful, graceful birds flew overhead.

Jesus was telling stories, and the children were laughing. As He saw us approach, He waved to my stepson, and said, "Come here, I've saved a place for you." Cole ran up to Jesus and sat on His lap. Jesus held him close, looked into his eyes, and said, "I've been waiting for you. I've got a place for you right here in My arms. I've missed you, and I love you. I want you to know that you're safe and secure."

Our story continued with Jesus laughing and playing with the children, enjoying His time with them. With that image in mind, my son had little trouble going off to sleep.

Jesus is the kind of man who allows a child to feel safe, who does not exploit or use but rather loves, holds, nurtures, and encourages. In Matthew 18, He called a little child and had him stand with Him. Then He told the disciples that unless they changed and became like children, they would never enter the kingdom of heaven.

Jesus also taught that we have a powerful responsibility to train, lead, and guide our children. If we are to be real men, we're to be about the business of teaching our sons to be men and our daughters to be women of honor.

This, then, is the biblical man—created by God in His image to be in relationship with Him. Further, the biblical man recognizes that God created woman to complete and fulfill man in a pure and holy relationship, and that children are a gift to be loved and nurtured.

TAKE ACTION

1. In your own words, how was human sexuality affected by sin's coming into the world?

2. Jesus Christ is our example of biblical manhood. He is a friend who knows all your faults and still loves you anyway (Romans 5:8). What can we learn about how Jesus handled His sexuality in His relationships with others? Review the section "The Biblical Manhood of Jesus," and on a piece of paper list ways in which Jesus used his maleness to relate to men, women, and children. In what ways was Jesus tempted as you in being a man? Can you imagine Jesus being tempted sexually?

   How did Jesus use His relationship with His heavenly Father to cope with temptations?

3. How close to Jesus' view of women is your own?

4. Ask your wife (or the woman closest to you if you're not married) what five things you could do regularly to show her more honor.

5. If you are married, think about the last couple of times you had sex with your wife. Was the lovemaking a celebration of your relationship, or was it sex that left you wanting?

   Consider praying sometimes before, during, or after sex and inviting God to your celebration and praising Him for this wonderful gift. What would happen if you discussed this matter with your wife?

6

THE SPIRITUAL MAN

As we saw in the last chapter, the Bible clearly connects our sexuality to our spiritual life. But what is spiritual? Is it being kind and passive? Is it being pure in every thought and action? Does it mean we must never be tempted? Does it mean doing the American spiritual check list: quiet time, church, witnessing, prayer, and tithing?

The answers to those questions can be found in the Scriptures, of course. A brief study of two men who talked with Jesus gives us some clear answers.

TWO VERY DIFFERENT MEN

A Spiritual Man

Most of us would agree that Peter was a spiritual man. He was a real man, prone to fits of temper and impatience, and honest about his feelings. And though he was full of faults and sins, he was spiritual. As one of twelve close followers whom Christ Himself chose, Peter believed Christ was God in the flesh, and said so. Jesus honored Peter for that declaration (Matthew 16:16–19). Peter also was one of the three men closest to Jesus, and Christ depended on him a lot.

This same Peter, however, tried to talk Christ out of going to the cross. At that moment, Christ referred to him as Satan (Matthew 16:21–23). Peter walked on the water with Christ, a spiritual triumph. Then he doubted and in a panic began to drown, a spiritual failure. Peter told Christ he would never leave Him and hours later denied he even knew Him. Is this really a spiritual man?

Yes, Peter is the reality of the spiritual life—the ups and downs, the successes and failures. For the spiritual man is one who seeks after God, and though he fails at times because of his sins, he still desires to know and honor God.

Being spiritual is not something that can be measured. But we can define *spiritual*: to be spiritual means to be in relationship with God. Peter was spiritual because he was in relationship with Christ, period.

"Love the Lord your God with all your heart, soul, and mind, and then love your neighbor as yourself" (see Luke 10:27–28). That is what matters. You are spiritual if you are in a relationship with God, seeking to please Him. No matter how well you measure up to your own standards or those of a church, you are spiritual when you seek to please God and walk in fellowship with Him. The key measure of spirituality, Jesus told the lawyer in Luke 10, is how your relationship with God affects your relationships with other people.

Like Peter, David did not do his relationships perfectly—the fractured relationship with his son Absalom and his deceit with Uriah (Bathsheba's husband) are prime examples—but he was willing to change. He could see his failures and use them in his relationship with God. He did not pretend to have it all together. Peter and David were spiritual men, so unlike the rich young man.

A Hypocritical Man

The rich young man in Matthew 19 seemingly had his life together, yet he would not be considered spiritual. He did everything right. He was religious. If he were part of the church today, he could say to Christ, "I go to church three times a week, I have daily quiet time, I memorize the Bible, I give my ten percent, I volunteer for every church event." Christ might reply back, "You lack one thing, a relationship with Me based on grace, not works."

The rich young man looked spiritual, but inside he was not willing to change, not willing to see himself clearly, and not willing to be in a relationship with all it would require.

Whole Spirituality

In our relationships with God and with women in our lives (our wives, or if unmarried, our girlfriends) real spirituality consists of having a consistent relationship that includes the *whole* person—the physical, mental, emotional, and spiritual. So when we speak of spiritual sexuality, we're saying that our sexuality is just as involved with our spiritual life as our mind is in how we treat ourselves and the women with whom we have deep relationships. In fact, what we do with our sexuality is as spiritual as going to church or praying.

Spirituality is not independent from our mind and spirit, nor is it independent from our physical self. There is a tendency to separate the physical from the spiritual, but this split is actually unhealthy for true spirituality. Both the Hollywood Man and the Church Man separate their sexuality from their spiritual life.

Now, if spirituality is a relationship with God, it involves communication, feelings, conflict, time, and commitment. In spiritual sexuality we discuss our sexuality with God. We feel our frustration, anger, joy, and other feelings with God. Yes, in our honesty we may have conflicts with God, and our conflicts can involve our sexuality. He is willing to listen to us and respond; He wants to help us with our sexual urges.

On the other hand, if we have great difficulties in the arena of sexuality, we can't always point to a spiritual problem. Our sexual struggles can be connected to our spiritual lives, but just as often our spiritual lives can be our only source of strength to deal with those problems.

SEXUAL INSIGHT

SPIRITUAL GROWTH AND SEX

Developing your spiritual being will benefit your sexual being, whether you are single or married. Here are five ways that spiritual growth can aid your sexual life. Remember, as whole beings, our spiritual, emotional, and physical being affects our sexuality.

1. *Helps you focus on love and friendship in the relationship.* We men can be deluded into thinking that the essence of a romantic relationship is sex. But the relationship should also emphasize love and friendship. In fact, these two elements are more important and contribute to sexual interest.

If you are single, choose to value the emotional and spiritual elements of the relationship over your physical interest. This contributes to increasing knowledge of the other person, which can help you in understanding whether you desire the relationship to deepen. If you are married, remember that your relationship has a priority over sex. When you love your wife, you will always place her need above your sexual desires; that is love in action, to "consider others better than yourselves" (Philippians 2:3). There may even be times when sex is not possible, because of physical or emotional problems. During such times we can choose to love each other in a way that is based on grace and caring.

2. *Helps you deal with rejection in your sex life, by allowing God to work through your pain.* When we are turned down romantically, we cannot always know the reason. But we can go to God to discuss the pain and allow Him to comfort us. God can teach us many things when a romantic relationship dissolves, and He can prepare us for new relationships that will build on past ones.

If you're married, realize that your wife may reject your sexual overtures for legitimate reasons. Such rejection may feel painful, and you may feel angry or frustrated. As you allow God to love you, however, you can risk a discussion with your wife about her reason not to engage in sexual relations. You will often discover her choice is not a reflection on you as a man or husband but the result of an issue she is dealing with at the time. Something as simple as a bad day with the children can make her unprepared for lovemaking. Here's a great opportunity to be a friend by listening to her day and giving loving comfort.

3. *Gives healthy boundaries to your sexuality.* God's limits to our sexuality are for our welfare. The single man has the opportunity to focus on the spiritual and emotional needs of the woman he is with, without complicating the relationship with deep sexual involvement. Sexual expression is appropriate (see chapter 8 for further discussion of single sexuality), but the boundaries a man establishes to protect the woman's purity are expressions of love and respect.

The married man also must recognize certain limits. Though new sexual techniques may add variety, we must watch out for anything that makes our wives feel uncomfortable or degraded. We must also avoid any sexual temptations outside marriage that may cause our marriage pain and call our faithfulness into question. Marriage is a place where real trust can be built. Trust will promote honest communication and a willingness to work out conflicts. A good relationship—and good sex—are symptoms of true commitment.

4. *Permits your risking open, honest communication with your wife about your sexual desires.* As we study Christ's life, we will find guidelines and encouragement in improving our communication skills. Christ consistently demonstrated honesty in communicating his emotions, from anger at the Pharisee leaders, to grief over the death of a friend, to revealing his personal pain to an inner circle of followers while in the garden of Gethsemane. His example can motivate us to risk our real feelings about our sexual desires and needs with our wives. Without taking such risks our wives will not understand who we are and how we view our sexuality. By letting our wives enter our lives by openly communicating our feelings, we eliminate our frustrations regarding our sexual fears and wants and their frustrations at not being allowed near our pain, our real self.

5. *Imparts God's view of sex.* When we feed our spiritual being, we bring proper perspective to our sexual being. We see sex as it truly is: something God created for our benefit. God intended our sexuality to be something we could thank Him for and He wants us to enjoy. This is the only antidote to the warped thinking of the Hollywood Man and the Church Man. When we have God's perspective, we have a healthy view of our sexuality. We see sex as complementing our relationships, not the focus of our relationships. We can trust that our sexual desires are given by God and instilled to drive us to healthy relationships.

Suggested Reading

Bill Hybels and Rob Wilkins, *Tender Love* (Chicago: Moody, 1993).

Lewis B. Smedes, *Sex for the Christian* (Grand Rapids, Mich: Eerdmans, 1976).

How to Integrate—or Separate— Our Spirituality in Marriage

Just how our sexual, emotional and spiritual dimensions can integrate with each other can be seen in the stories of Don and Bob. Don eventually linked his spirituality with the rest of his being. In contrast, Bob shelved his spirituality while at home with his wife.

Don was a patient who struggled with impotence, the inability to achieve or keep an erection sufficient for intercourse. Clearly his impotence was not a result of physical problems; he had erections during the night and his penis became very hard if he masturbated.

Don's Story

Don and his wife, Rebecca, had been somewhat sexually active before their marriage but had refrained from intercourse. Their dating life had been romantic and passionate. They were looking forward to a great marriage and a great sex life. Don had always been a sensitive man and desired with all his heart to love his wife as Christ loved the church. To Don that meant sacrificial love. He had spent his married life trying to show such love.

As Don reported during a counseling session, however, "My motives were not quite as pure as they looked. I seldom expressed my true feelings and held resentment inside. I felt like I did all the sacrificing. To ensure there would be no conflict in the marriage, I did not ask for my needs to be met and became very passive in the relationship. These communication problems and relationship patterns were creating emotional distance and unresolved anger."

As a result, he found himself impotent. He felt that God would remove the problem if he had enough faith; he had not recognized the need to deal with the underlying issues.

"I really wanted God to give me sexual desire for Rebecca without having to deal with the underlying issues and relationship patterns. My sexual problems were not a result of a spiritual problem or a lack of faith. My problems were related to how I dealt with being vulnerable and working out the conflicts."

In truth, Don had a strong faith and would be considered a spiritual man. He had a real relationship with God and spent quality time with Him. Thus, Don's sexual struggle was not a result of a spiritual struggle with God. Instead, he wrestled with fear of being vulnerable before his wife. How Don chose to deal with those struggles, however, became spiritual. Though Don believed he "was deeply loved by God even with those struggles—God's love was not conditional on my sexual performance or my faith," the real issue was his passive-dependent relationship with Rebecca. He faced an underlying spiritual dilemma. "The spiritual issue was trusting God to help me to be open and honest with my wife."

As Don began to trust God with his real feelings and started to discuss the problems with Rebecca, things began to change. In Don's case, spirituality was his source of strength. He needed to trust that with God's help, he could handle the conflict and possible rejection. Don came to believe God is faithful and will be there for us when we take a risk. Like Peter, he was willing to change, to see his mistakes and take a chance.

Don realized, "My idea of sacrificial love had to change. Real sacrificial love is communicating your deepest feelings and risking rejection. I learned that assertiveness does not mean being selfish."

Bob's Story

In Bob's case, it was not difficult to detect what was going on in his marriage. He was acting like the rich young man. He had it all together; his wife, Sue, was messed up. They had what he called a great sex life, but she felt lonely and doubted she wanted to stay in the marriage. As we probed deeper, we found out that Sue felt used in the sexual relationship.

Bob would say to her, "The Bible says the wife should not deprive her husband of sex." Even if Sue was feeling down or sick, Bob would tell her, "If you really love me, you will never deprive me." He required her to have sex nightly or at least four times a week. He also seemed to have a great need for different styles of sex and wanted Sue to do things she found uncomfortable. He was not willing to talk with her about these problems until Sue told him she was not interested in sex anymore.

Sue explained, "The only time I heard Bob tell me he loved me was during sex. He would tell me he would pray for me. He looked spiritual, going to church and reading his Bible, saying all the right words. Bob seemed very content in the marriage and could not understand my problems. I was seldom satisfied in the sexual arena but was afraid to tell Bob."

Sadly, Bob had left his spirituality outside the marriage. He knew the Scriptures—he had a lot of head knowledge—but his sexuality was not spiritual. Bob had been able to deny his wife true intimacy yet convince her she needed to be sexually involved with him. He was not sinning in where or who he was having sex with, but he was sinning in how he expressed his sexuality. There was a spiritual problem here! Bob had disconnected the sexual relationship from the emotional and spiritual. He was manipulating his wife and even using the Scriptures to do so. His concern was not for her spiritual and emotional growth. Instead, he had regarded his sexual needs independently from the sexual and spiritual needs of his wife. The result was a marriage relationship that did not model God's love to his wife, which is itself a sin.

Male sexuality does not exist in a void; it is connected to our relationship with God in some profound ways. On the other hand, we do not want to fall prey to spiritualizing sex to such an extent that sexual problems are always a spiritual dilemma. There is a balance to spiritual sexuality. Let's look at a framework that gives us this biblical balance.

THE IMAGE OF GOD

Human beings are created in the image of God. This image is tarnished by sin, but the foundations of the image are still present. So what? Understanding this image gives us a framework to understand what it means to be a man. Apart from this image, we can put aside the majority of our discussion and simply say the purpose of sex is to reproduce. But the image lets us know that like God, we're to be emotional, intellectual, spiritual, and relational. Let's look at each of those aspects in turn.

Emotional

The Bible reveals that God feels anger, jealousy, joy, sadness, and many other emotions. We might think that Christ was emotional just because He was human, but the reality is that God is emotional and Christ is the perfect image of God in human flesh. In fact, of all the men in the Bible, Christ was one of the most emotional. He was open to his feelings but was not controlled by them. Consider Christ at Lazarus's grave; He wept openly. Christ under a tree with children around Him and on His lap: He showed joy with them and perhaps laughed aloud. Christ at the temple: in a display of controlled anger, He chased the moneychangers from their stations so the place could remain a house of worship. Christ in the garden of Gethsemane: He grieved His coming separation from God and perspired heavily as He anguished over the loss He would suffer.

As a carpenter and teacher, Christ was among the most manly of men. Yet He freely displayed His emotions. As we model our lives after Jesus, we too should grow in our ability to open up about our feelings.

American men think that emotions are feminine, but in reality, men have strong feelings that our culture teaches them to deny or to push deep inside. This is a distortion of the image of God. Emotions give life power! What we do with our emotions can affect our physical health, our ability to build relationships, and even our sex life.

In the movie *Big*, actor Tom Hanks plays a twelve-year-old in an adult body. Interestingly, Hanks's character is actually more mature than his adult co-workers. That's because he is in touch with his feelings. He's not afraid to be himself, so he's able to relate to people in healthy ways.

While watching the movie, I (Rick) felt a great deal of pain. I realized that inside, I felt very much like a twelve-year-old. I had been able to deny my feelings for years. As my wife and I discussed my reaction, tears began to flow. Boy, did I feel childish! My wife's acceptance of my feelings and the discussion brought us very close that night. Part of what I realized is that I can feel and that when I do, I feel like a child. But those feelings are not childish, they're just real, and they don't take away from my masculinity. They actually build intimacy in my marriage.

A quality communication pattern with our wives will involve our feelings and our willingness to consider our wives' emotions. We need to communicate our fears about our wives' sexual needs. We need to understand our own sexual needs and wants. We must comprehend the difference between feeling sexual and the expression of those feelings. We will certainly benefit from the ability to communicate our desires and not expect our spouses to read our minds.

The blocking of hurt or angry feelings can produce a lack of sexual desire, as we've seen. But working through problems and sharing our feelings develop love. This love moves us toward our spouse in healthy ways.

Intellectual

Our God thinks, creates, and makes decisions. We were made to do the same. Our ability to think can help in expressing our emotions in productive ways. We can learn to think properly about male sexuality, and we can get educated about women and the details of marital sex. We can evaluate our culture in light of God's Word, and we can understand how to live and apply biblical principles to a variety of problems. We can evaluate the messages we received growing up and choose to tell ourselves the truth.

Ken finally used his mind to think through issues after he discovered he had been wrong in his assumptions about how his wife viewed sex. "I believed that sex would just come naturally in my marriage," he told me one afternoon. "I always assumed my wife thought about sex the way I did and thought she was wrong if she regarded sex differently. As a result, I often felt angry and rejected in my marriage.

"I began to use my mind to read a book on sexuality. I quickly realized she did not think about sex the way I did. I tended to base our marriage on our sex life, but the book showed how women see sex as a small part of the marriage relationship. By thinking differently about our sex life, I began to be more comfortable with the differences between men and women."

Ken was using his mind to transform how he viewed sex. How we think influences how we feel. Ken often felt angry that his wife viewed sex so differently; as he understood these differences the anger lost its power.

We are created to use our minds. When we use our ability to think we can evaluate our feelings and not allow them to overwhelm us. We live in a society that continually tells us what to think about ourselves, about love, and about sex. What is true? As Christians, we have a valuable resource: a renewed mind that can help us discern truth. Our battle is largely spiritual, letting God's truth dominate over the myths of a society largely without God. Gary Oliver says men who want to make the right decisions about their identity and behavior must recognize the mind is a spiritual battleground and need to fill it with biblical truth.

> The major battleground for spiritual warfare is the mind. Part of being made in God's image means that we have a mind. Our mind is the seat of reflective consciousness and performs activities such as perceiving, thinking, problem-solving, remembering, learning, and choosing and experiencing thoughts and emotions. . . .
>
> The mind is the place that decisions are made for or against the truth. . . . God wants to help our minds become more like the mind of Christ.[1]

We can use our minds to learn the truth about spiritual issues and sexual issues. We need a critical thinking process to evaluate sexuality from a Christlike mindset. As Paul urges us, "Do not conform any longer to the pattern of this world, but be transformed by the renewing of your mind. Then you will be able to test [think critically] and approve what God's will is—his good, pleasing and perfect will" (Romans 12:1–2).

Spiritual

We are created as spiritual beings; we need relationship with God to be fully alive. We're not just physical animals who make up this belief in God to alleviate our fears of nature. The spiritual life is connected to the mysterious. We cannot fully understand God. Our sexual life is also a mystery.

Being in a relationship with God gives us purpose and moral direction. This choice to be related to Him calls us to a higher plane of living. There is more to life than our desires and fulfillment. We were created to know and be known by God. We cannot leave our sexuality out of the relationship. God is not embarrassed by these issues and is more than willing to work with us.

Though we don't earn God's love, we need to put ourselves in a place where He can meet us. One of the driest spiritual times in my life was at the end of an eight-year involvement in ministry. I was back in seminary working on my counseling degree. While in the ministry, I had been highly consistent in my devotions, church attendance, and evangelism. Now I felt burned out. I was angry at the church for not being more Christian and not being the perfect family for me. I was angry that life was hard and felt dry spiritually.

Now I see this time as God maturing me. I was learning how to love Him in a completely different way. God met me and conveyed His love unconditionally. I realized I no longer needed to earn that love. At times I still struggle to accept God's unconditional love. But in that struggle my sexual life has benefited. Clearly the spiritual element of our lives affects every other. For me, the spiritual struggle has revealed how conditional at times my love was for my wife. Depending on how she treated me, how she performed as a wife and mother, and on her desire for sex, I would respond with love or the withholding of love.

As I learn of God's acceptance, I grow in my ability to accept my wife where she is at. God is patient with our slow growth. You may not always be close to Him, but He desires your fellowship and will supply your needs (1 Peter 5:7). As we learn about God and model our spiritual lives after the example of Christ, forgiveness, grace, compassion, and respect will characterize our sexual lives. We will understand that sex is part of the relationship and not the primary determinant of the state of our marriage.

Relational

Our God is a triune God—God the Father, God the Son, and God the Holy Spirit communicate and are in perfect relationship. We were likewise created to be in relationship. We can't know who we are apart from it.

It has been said no one knows us like our families; our parents, brothers, and sisters have spent years living with us and know us well. However, if you are married, your wife probably knows you better, as she sees most aspects of your life and, unlike your parents and siblings, is *now* living with you. In marriage the best and the worst of who we are is played out. In fact, like our relationship with God, when we look at ourselves in terms of our relationship with our wives, we often see our utter selfishness. Yet in that human relationship, as in our relationship with God, we are reminded that we are deeply loved by God and forgiven, and in the process of becoming Christlike.

Though single men do not experience this particular human relationship, they too can learn about themselves—their selfishness as well as their potential for love and wholeness—through committed friendships with other men and women. The way single or married people relate to others is at the same time a reflection of their sexuality and their spirituality.

As writer and professor Lewis Smedes puts it,

> This brings us to sexuality in God's image. Sexuality is the human drive toward intimate communion. Beyond the glandular impulse, the human sexual urge is always towards another person. We want to experience the other, to trust the other and be trusted by him, to enter the other's life by entering the vital embrace of his/her body. . . . Having said that sexuality is a drive that begins in our glands and climaxes in communion, we now add that personal communion is what the image of God is about. Biblical revelation tells us to stop thinking of ourselves as isolated islands of rational God-likeness and think of ourselves instead as coming into real humanity when we live in genuine personal fellowship with others. A single person is in the image of God; but he is God's image only when he personally relates in love to others.[2]

We cannot understand ourselves sexually outside of relationships with women and healthy male friendships. The way we relate is a reflection of the image of God.

Bob, who demanded frequent sexual performance from his wife, Sue, had separated sex from his marital relationship; thus he had separated sex from his relational and spiritual being. He was using sex to feel comforted and loved. He did not listen to his wife or try to understand her needs but was using her the way men use prostitutes.

In our culture, the Hollywood Man and the Church Man in many ways have reduced sexuality to the physical and romantic part of our lives. This compartmentalizing of our lives separates sex from God, from communication, from a growing relationship, and even from developing male friendships. The ability to separate sex from relationship is a result of the Fall of mankind. But through God's grace in sending His Son to redeem men and women, we now can find restoration to wholeness in our being. And this is the foundation of our displaying truth and grace in our relationships.

Truth and Grace

Our growth in spiritual sexuality will be a product of both truth and grace in our lives. Many men struggle to find a balance between the two. Some of us get caught up in the works of the Christian life and miss the truth. We become modern Pharisees who believe we're great Christians because we don't have any major sexual sin in our lives. The reality is that we have just as much sin and self-justification as the next man struggling with sexual issues. Others are caught up in truth, knowing Scripture but not accepting God's grace for ourselves. Instead, they recall sins that God has already forgotten about. And sometimes we do not show grace through compassion and forgiveness of our wives. Let's see how truth and grace should work together.

Truth

Truth comes from knowing who God is. God is holy. At the same time, some of us seem to have forgotten that Christ died for us while we sinners (Romans 5:8). I have found a complacency in my own Christian life because of an attitude that the truth is for others who have more serious problems. In reality, that's the same type of sin Adam and Eve started off with—self-sufficiency. So what truths must we know to bring balance to our sexuality?

The truth is that we live in a fallen world, and this world will never work for us. We will never be satisfied or complete. Among other things, this means there is no such thing as perfect sex. There is no such thing as the perfect woman. The perfect marriage is a myth from Hollywood. Romance, the movie type, lasts six months to a year in most marriages. Marital romance must be worked at and created. Sex is something we can talk about and improve on because it doesn't come naturally. We will be tempted to make sex into an idol, something that will bring meaning and some sort of everlasting joy. But sex cannot meet those deep spiritual needs. Sex is an enjoyable experience but should not be the top priority of marriage.

The truth is that sex was intended to be enjoyed within the boundaries of marriage. That's not some out-of-date notion. As noted at the end of chapter 2, a 1986 Masters and Johnson report on human sexuality found that the people who did have an affair found the sex in their marriages more satisfying. And recent surveys by the National Opinion Research Center found that only 15 percent of married people have affairs (see page 29, Self Test answer 1.).

We have a self-fulfilling prophecy in American society that says men cannot resist premarital sex and that abstinence is too high a standard for normal people. The truth, however, is that men can and many men do choose to wait until they're married to have sex. This is not a negative reflection on their masculinity.

Healthy sex takes commitment. In a growing relationship, the chances of a good sex life are much improved. The opposite is also true: in a relationship with limited communication, emotional contact, and commitment, sex often is disappointing and frustrating.

Sexual sin will create hurtful consequences and spiritual pain. The truth is we cannot disconnect our sexual expression from our spiritual life.

Grace

God loves us. Through faith in Christ, we cannot escape God's acceptance. This type of love is life changing. It can have supernatural power in our lives and heal others. The church was founded on this grace, yet today, many local churches tend to emphasize works to grace, in part because works are easier to measure. As Brennan Manning writes in *The Ragamuffin Gospel,*

> The institutional church has become a wounder of the healers rather than a healer of the wounded. . . . Something is radically wrong when the local church rejects a person accepted by Jesus: when a harsh, judgmental and unforgiving sentence is passed on homosexuals; when a divorcée is denied communion; when the child of a prostitute is refused baptism; when an unlaicized priest is forbidden the sacraments. Jesus comes to the ungodly, even on Sunday morning. His coming ends ungodliness and makes us worthy. Otherwise, we are establishing at the heart of Christianity an utterly ungodly and unworthy preoccupation with works.
>
> Jesus sat down at table with anyone who wanted to be present, including those who were banished from decent homes. In the sharing of a meal they received consideration instead of the expected condemnation. A merciful acquittal instead of a hasty verdict of guilty. Amazing grace instead of universal disgrace. Here is a very practical demonstration of the law of grace—new chance in life.[3]

The truth is that grace is yours if you are a follower of Christ. He gives us a new chance at life.

Men who struggle with sexual sin will find grace's healing power sufficient. Well-meaning but mistaken Christians who condemn those who have fallen in sexual sins have created false condemnation; men have felt incredible guilt and shame. Grace, the first step in the healing process, is yours if you have stumbled in your sexual past. Grace means acceptance for who you are and a restored position in God's eyes.

This is not cheap grace, however. This type of grace, like that shown through the cross when God provided a way back to Him, helps to move a person out of sinful patterns. Truly accepting God's love often will create confusion in men who have previously gained approval by performance. They may wonder if there is something more they can do. There is not, for everything has been done by Christ. Our response to this love, however, is to "go and sin no more" (John 8:11), seeking to live to please our Father. Grace motivates; the law and works immobilize.

Grace is the foundation in the building of a Christian man. To be a true man of integrity, we must first admit that in ourselves we have little integrity. Grace is known as we understand God's holiness as well as His choice to love us and provide the means to redeem us. He alone can make us whole, integrated men.

Grace allows us to move away from our sins. We need safe places in our lives to develop healthy sexuality. Grace-based relationships can provide those places. Loving someone in spite of his continuing in sin begins the process of change. As husbands, we also can exhibit such grace in learning about and accepting our wives. We will desire to meet their needs above our own. As single men, we can exhibit grace in accepting the women we date, affirming them and enjoying their company, all the while respecting and encouraging their virginity in anticipation of the day they may marry.

Grace is how God loves us. It is how we should love ourselves and the women in our lives.

Truth and grace fit hand in hand in developing your spiritual sexuality. Truth provides the boundaries for healthy relationships. Grace gives us the ability to be transformed and the forgiveness to move on. Truth helps us see the lies in the Hollywood Man and the Church Man. Grace allows for a process of working our way through those lies. Truth calls us to purity in thought, word, and action. Grace calls us to passion and deep love. Together, these two elements of the Christian life provide men with balance and guidance in having spiritual sexuality.

TAKE ACTION

1. How do you define the word *spiritual?* Do you consider yourself spiritual? List at least three ways you are spiritual.

2. How does God regard you; what would He say to you about your sexuality?
   Do you feel safe discussing your sex life with God? Why or why not?

3. Is your tendency to be too legalistic or too free? What would you give a friend struggling with sexual sin, truth or grace? Why?

4. List three ways in which a fresh appreciation of God's grace might help you in your sexual struggles.

7

MAN TO MAN

Close friendships contribute to a healthy male sexuality.

Yes, it's true that if we have close friends, our sex lives stand a much better chance of being good. That may sounds crazy, but I'm convinced it's true for a number of reasons. Men with close male friends will feel less dependent on women. Instead, they have a helpful sounding board with a true male perspective. They can express their anger and vent other feelings without offense. If married, they will not expect too much from their wives, as another friend is available to listen to their concerns. Furthermore, a male friend can provide a better response when it comes to understanding certain male issues, including our sexual feelings.

Good male friends will participate in honest, frank discussion of sexual desires and needs. As a result, our expectations of sex will not be as high, for we can see our misconceptions and discuss our fears in a nonthreatening setting. A true friend will help carry the struggles involved in singleness and in marriage. In short, real strength is found in the body of Christ when Christian men commit to friendships with one another.

Christ picked three close friends, Peter, James, and John, and focused on them. We also need to focus on a few male friends and mature those relationships. Closeness requires more than attending the same church.

We would like friendships to happen naturally, as they seemed to do when we were kids, but we know that's not realistic. When we think about all that we do already, however, adding a friendship to our schedules feels a bit overwhelming. How come friendships are so hard to come by? And what can we do to develop them?

In My Father's Image

We learn about man-to-man relationships from our fathers and how they treated us. We also learn by how our fathers handled their friendships.

For a moment, picture the family room of your childhood home. What's going on? Where is your father sitting, and where are you sitting? What does the conversation revolve around? Who is doing most of the talking? How old are you in this memory?

Now try to remember the best memory you have of a time with your dad. What are the two of you doing? Who else is involved? Why is this your favorite memory?

Finally, try to recall your worst memory of your father. What's happening? Why is this time so painful?

Answering those questions will help you understand who you are today. Even how we (or our decision not to) form male friendships are affected by our experiences with our dads. Our fathers directly and indirectly influence who we are; for that reason, homes without fathers early on, through death or divorce, affect the sons' attitudes and future relationships to men. Think again about your memories. Two questions we want to answer are: How do those memories relate to your male friendships? How are your friendships like and unlike your relationship with your dad?

To begin to answer those questions, let's look at four kinds of fathers. As we look at several stories of typical father-son relationships, we will learn how particular fathers can affect a son's need for and ability to make friends.

The Absentee Father

"I never thought my father was any different from any other father, and maybe he wasn't. My father did the best he could."

Dean, a forty-year-old father of three and married twenty years, came to my counseling office after realizing his need for a close friend and feeling unable to find one. He described his father as a diligent worker. "He worked hard in sales to provide his family the best that money could buy. My dad tried to make it to the sporting events I was in when the time was available. We spent the weekends working around the house and catching games on TV."

Then Dean acknowledged "something was missing" from his father's life. "I wasn't sure what it was, I just felt a distance between the two of us. My dad was an absentee father not because he wasn't around but because when he was around, he wasn't present. My dad avoided the topics of life and meaning. We didn't talk about failures, puberty, women, or sex.

"I guess my father modeled emotional distance. He did not discuss his fears or his feelings toward his son and wife. We didn't talk to each other about our relationship.

"My father had friends, but these friendships revolved around sports and church. I saw my father relate to men on a level of facts. Their discussions were around business, the business of church, sports, and sales.

"I always wanted to develop close friendships but found the process confusing. I needed to understand that my tendency is to repeat the patterns of my father."

If your father was like Dean's, he modeled emotional distance. There is safety in such emotional distance. This model sets you up to struggle with true intimacy, however. Your tendency is to become an absentee friend. You may have a lot of friends, but the friendships are superficial.

If you grew up with an absentee father, you probably believe:

1. Men don't have emotions and don't need other men in their lives.
2. Work is more important than friendships.
3. Friendships need to revolve around work and be beneficial to your work.
4. It's best to avoid conflict with your spouse and friends.
5. Your father and mother seldom had sex and probably didn't enjoy it.

6. Commitment to friendships might be going too far.
7. Discussing sexual issues with a friend is too personal.

Though you probably believe commitment to friendships is "going too far," a friend is what you need. If you had an absentee father, a close friend would be a safe place to go deeper. A friend could challenge you to be more assertive and could help you discuss your sexual issues. A good friend would open up to you and allow you to be yourself. You would learn that many men struggle with similar sexual issues. A good friend could help you lower your expectations of sex and be less emotionally dependent on a girlfriend or wife.

The Overinvolved Father

Sam's father was too involved in his life. He coached the Little League team and came to every school function. He discussed all his personal problems with Sam and asked for his advice. Sam's dad would question Sam about his buddies and tell him whom he could hang out with.

Sam's performance on the field felt like his dad's performance. He thought he owed his dad a great deal. Sam often heard, "My son is the best. He deserves better treatment than that. . . . No son of mine would say things like that. I will talk to your teacher about that and fix it for you. . . . You're too good for that girl or those friends. . . . Son, what do you think I should do about your sister?"

Sam remembers, "I felt a great deal of shame and guilt when I failed. I felt I was not failing myself but was failing Dad. I believed Dad's problems were my problems. I felt responsible for how he felt about himself. I knew Dad loved me, but I felt smothered. I wanted to take responsibility for my own life."

When Sam was in high school, his dad sat down with him to talk about sex. Sam got the first degree. Instead of discussing the issues, pitfalls, and challenges of Sam's sexuality, his father wanted to know all about Sam's sex life. Sam didn't want to discuss details, but eventually he told his dad about what he was doing. What Sam received for his honesty was shame and a "How could you after all I've done for you?"

What Sam's dad actually modeled was insecurity and low self-esteem. He was living his life through Sam.

If you were raised by an overinvolved father, you will struggle with male friendships. Like Sam, you find the thought of being close to a male friend burdensome, not a relief. Here are some of the results of being raised by an overinvolved father:

1. You find yourself getting used in your friendships.
2. You end up feeling responsible for everyone's feelings.
3. You find you have little time for yourself.
4. You feel guilty about not caring enough for people.
5. You end up overinvolved in activities with friends.
6. You struggle asking your friends for special time.
7. You might fear getting close to another male.

Men with overinvolved fathers also need male friends. A good friend will help such men learn about healthy boundaries, about being close but not dependent. If you're the son of an overinvolved father, realize that a good friend can help you understand your responsibility for the sexual relationship. Such a friend can be independent of you yet still desire a close relationship. If you're married, such a friend can help you take your marriage struggles less seriously and enjoy the good aspects of your sexual life. He could help you find the balance between time with family and time for yourself.

THE ABUSIVE FATHER

Nick entered group therapy with a distrust for all men. His first night in group, he picked a verbal fight with another group member. He stated, "I don't need a group, and I don't believe a word of what Rick [the therapist] is saying." By the end of that first session, however, he was challenged by his lack of close male friends.

Five group meetings later, Nick broke down in tears while discussing the physical and verbal abuse he had received from his father. His father would refer to him as the "thing" and would use the littlest mistake as an excuse to slap him across the face.

Nick had no clue as to how to relate to men. On the outside he was the tough guy, while on the inside, he was a scared little boy needing the love and affirmation of male friends.

Did you grow up with an abusive father? There are three kinds of abuse many boys experience. The first is physical abuse, which can range from being slapped in the face to receiving bruises and cuts. Many of us think we deserved this treatment and find it difficult to call it abuse.

The second type of abuse is verbal. Being called stupid over and over again will create emotional damage. Verbal abuse includes messages like "You're worthless." "If it weren't for you, I would be happy." "I'm going to shoot you in the head."

The third type of abuse is neglect. This includes not meeting a child's basic physical needs. Neglect would be when a father (or mother) leaves young children alone in a house. Some fathers don't act as if the child is even alive, ignoring him completely.

If you grew up in an abusive home, just the thought of discussing sex with your father created fear. You may have heard abusive things said about women and sex. You could believe sex is a way to solve your anger.

An abusive father often displays abuse in the marital relationship. He views women as objects, including your mother. Sex is a symbol of masculinity; love is a sign of weakness. If you grew up in an abusive home, you might struggle with:

1. Trusting male friends with your deeper feelings.
2. Moving sexual conversations beyond locker-room jokes.
3. Communicating your love for a friend.
4. Seeing women as sex objects.
5. Being abusive with your own wife and children.
6. Friendships that are kept on the surface to avoid anger and competition.

You also need a male friend. Men from abusive homes need male friends to help them deal with their sexuality. Friends can hold you accountable as you deal with your anger—and you will feel angry. They can give you new ways to see women. They can talk with you about their struggles in the sexual area and how they deal with them.

The Nurturing Father

The nurturing father is the father many men would like to have had. He is not abusive, yet he can be a disciplinarian. He is willing to talk about any subject and would allow you to have your opinion. He spent quantity and quality time with you. He treated your mother with respect and love. He would admit when he failed. A nurturing father was comfortable expressing his feelings and was appropriately affectionate with you.

Barry recalls his father as a nurturing man. "I remember when Dad found me exploring my genitals," he says. "He did not act embarrassed or angry. He just noticed what I was doing and a day later sat down to talk with me about masturbation. He described how sex was a creation of God and told me about the balance to sexuality and exploration. This gentle conversation created an atmosphere of safety. I felt comfortable going to my dad with sexual questions. I really believe this openness on my dad's part helped me control my sexual life while I remained single and then feel comfortable with sex in my marriage."

The nurturing father did not give the "sex talk" and then close the subject. He continued to discuss puberty and sexual issues as you grew up. You would feel comfortable asking him about sex and his sexual life. In his honesty, he would usually admit when he failed, but he would treat your mother with respect and love. And he was affectionate with you in appropriate ways.

If you grew up with a nurturing father, you would:

1. Have two or three close friends.
2. Feel comfortable discussing sex and your sex life with your friends.
3. Find that friends trust you with personal information.
4. Keep personal information about a friend to yourself.
5. Have lasting friendships that involve mutual commitment.
6. Find time to talk and meet with your friends regularly.
7. Realize your struggles in the sexual area are common to the majority of men.

Men who have nurturing fathers find their male friends necessary for mutual accountability. You need male friendships to keep your perspective. Your expectations of friendship would be realistic. You need friends to push you toward excellence and listen to your deep feelings. You realize your spouse cannot meet all your needs. You find yourself working at finding the balance between your family and a couple of quality friendships where you are totally honest and risk discussing the tough subjects.

OUR FATHERS' VIEW OF SEX

Our fathers' perspective on sex continues to influence our view. Many men tell me they have no idea how their fathers felt about sex. But even though our fathers didn't say much, they gave us messages in a multitude of ways. We can look back and recall small things that indicate how they saw sex.

George felt confused by this thing called sex. His father was an absentee dad. George always respected him for his hard work and success. George received his "sex talk" from Dad at age thirteen. George's father took him to a restaurant one evening. George seldom went out to eat alone with dad, so the evening was already a bit unusual. They spent the first hour talking about sports and business stuff.

Near the end of the meal, George's dad said, "Son, I wanted to talk to you about sex." He went on to explain awkwardly how sex worked. George recalls, "I was completely surprised by how difficult this was for my dad. Everything my dad talked about I had known for two years. My dad did not talk about personal issues regarding sex. It was as if sex was only a biological function. When the lecture was over, my dad asked, 'Any questions?' When I said no, he finished with, 'Good.'"

The messages George picked up had more impact than the information. He learned that this successful father was insecure discussing sex. He realized the topic of sex as a conversation was over. "I picked up that sex was a function that men did. I wanted to talk to my dad about petting and how to deal with women, but he seemed uncomfortable."

George went through high school and part of college never discussing sex with his father. He was raised on the romantic myths of Hollywood. Now five years into his marriage, sex was just as confusing. It wasn't that he doesn't know what to do; it was what sex meant. He knew sex has more to it than just a physical release.

George began opening himself up to a good friend. "At first, I didn't know how to talk about sex other than telling a good joke now and then. But I risked looking like a fool and began to discuss the deeper meaning of sex. My friend was more than willing to talk about his concerns. This friendship helped me understand male sexuality in a whole new way. The spiritual issues were discussed. The confusion was talked about. The expectations were laughed at. Without this friendship, I may have taken sex out of the spiritual realm and at the same time taken sex too seriously."

The Power of a Secret

Our fathers struggled with the mystery and power of sex; they knew there was a lot they didn't understand. This created a communication gap, as it was safer not to discuss something they didn't have the answers for. Thus, the message many of us received from our fathers was sex is a secret. Instead, we needed to know that sex is a mystery and that Dad did not have all the answers, but that he cared and would give advice when he could. We also needed him to encourage us to honor women and come to him to talk when we needed to.

Secrets in our fathers' lives haunt us. History repeats itself. Consider Gary, who spent a year in an affair with the woman of his dreams. His wife found out about it, as all wives eventually do. Gary sought counseling to find out why all this had taken place.

Gary's father was very distant emotionally and physically. Gary always loved his father, and his memories were positive. Gary's dad died when Gary was twenty-six. He always regretted not knowing more about him. During this period of searching, Gary went home to talk to his mother and other relatives about his need for the perfect love.

Gary began discussing with his mom the past and his parents' marriage. "I learned that my father had been married before he met my mother," he told me. "This had been a family secret. My mother explained that my father had told her about this marriage but said that it was over. My mother did not realize that, in fact, her fiancé was still married during their courtship. My own mother was my father's affair. Dad had found the 'perfect love' in my mother. I was actually repeating the secret dad was able to keep."

As Gary's experience demonstrates, our fathers' secrets often repeat themselves in our lives. Over and over again, I find that men who have affairs have fathers who had affairs. One friend actually found out his mistress had the same name as his father's mistress. Coincidence, you say? More likely, it's the natural working out of a biblical principle: "I, the Lord your God, am a jealous God, punishing the children for the sin of the fathers to the third and fourth generation of those who hate me" (Exodus 20:5).

Your father's attitudes and behavior toward sex affect you; if you are a father, you have great potential for good—and bad—as you influence *your* son's (and daughter's) attitude toward their sexuality. This is the phenomenon of *generational sin*, the sins of the father often being passed on to the son and later your son's children. Our fathers' sins affect us many ways; a primary way is that we may repeat their actions ourselves.

ROADBLOCKS TO MALE FRIENDSHIPS

When my grandfather died, I was at a youth ministry conference. My father offered to fly me back for the funeral, but I didn't go. I thought the ministry, my job, was more important. My grandfather had lived a good and long life. I had all sorts of reasons for not going back—rationalizations, really. What I missed, however, was an opportunity to be with my father and express my love for him. I missed the chance to be in relationship with him at a painful time in his life. All this because work was more important.

Five years later, my friend Chris's father died. I was in a new career and had important meetings to go to when I got the news. Somewhere, however, I had learned the value of a good friend and canceled my meetings. Tears come to my eyes as I remember crying with Chris. He had been my friend for ten years, yet that night was the first time I told him I loved him. This is a sad commentary on male friendships. It took my best friend's dad dying for me to tell him I loved him. What is going on with us men when we don't understand how to communicate love with our friends?

Communication

Yet most men struggle with communication, the key element in developing a quality friendship. The reason is we have been reared in a society that models "strong" unemotional men as "real men." Growing up, I did not see an adult male show any emotion other than anger. Clint Eastwood was the perfect example of how to be a man. Clint's one emotion was calm, cool anger. His anger always came out in revenge.

In the first book in this Men of Integrity series, Gary Oliver wrote about the difficulty men have in expressing their feelings. Appropriately entitled *Real Men Have Feelings Too,* the book explains why men struggle to communicate. It's not because men dislike communication and emotions, according to Oliver. The problem is they have difficulty expressing feelings: "Men are emotional. The problem is that most men don't understand their emotions and they have not learned healthy and appropriate ways to express them (though they do express feelings in various ways)."[1]

The men I know have strong emotions, and they desire to express them in ways that work. The majority of men are more than willing to learn to be open and discuss their feelings. And it is a step we men must take in order to develop our relationships with other men.

We also close off potential communication because of fear of rejection as others find out who we are. Can a man show he is needy and still be accepted, or does society expect him to be independent and self-sufficient? As we have seen earlier, the myth of the self-contained Hollywood Man influences most of us. We are afraid to be vulnerable, a necessary quality if our male friends (and even our wives) are to help.

We also want to seem adequate spiritually and sexually, and in our drive to compete with other men, we may hesitate to communicate our needs and shortcomings. Indeed, competition and fear are among three other roadblocks to building strong friendships with men. The other, believe it or not, is women. Coming to grips with these three areas will enable us to build quality friendships that will enhance our lives and develop a healthier sexuality.

Competition

Competition is not an evil thing. Lively competition adds to life. I love a hard mountain bike ride with a group of guys, and there's always a sense of competition in those rides. Pushing each other, racing downhill, can add to the fun of friendships. I ride with one friend whom I will never get close to passing in an uphill climb. Sometimes I wish I could ride against him one day when he is really sick; it would just be fun to rub a victory in his face for once. This kind of competition is positive, and we men will always enjoy a little of it.

Other competition, however, is unhealthy. Men often compete for success, money, sexual experiences, and even spirituality, doing damage to themselves and their friendships. Money is one way that men in our culture have been conditioned to measure their worth. As Christians, we need to stay clear of this type of competition. Christ measures our worth on a different scale. We are worthwhile because we are human.

Comparing yourself to a friend who makes a lot of money also creates problems between the two of you. You can be jealous of him and envy him. You might find yourself seeing him as materialistic or greedy when the bad attitude is really yours. The apostle Paul issues repeated warnings against comparison and jealousy, saying a man should be content with what he has and not be "comparing himself to somebody else" and thus "deceive" himself (Galatians 6:3–4; see also Philippians 4:11–12).

Comparing your sexual life with someone else's can really mess up a friendship. If you are not careful, your desire to compete can make you brag or simply imply the sexual element of your marriage relationship is exotic and grand. Men often exaggerate in order to impress. Single men may do the same. The results are both dishonesty and the misleading implication that you do not struggle and need help and a listening ear about sexual issues. Furthermore, such exaggeration can set you or your friend up to expect more sex just to keep up with the Joneses. If you want a close friend, be honest about your struggles. Unfortunately, many men stretch the truth in an effort to affirm their masculinity.

Spiritual competition is not unusual among Christians. We try to measure spirituality by outward acts. This kind of competition can destroy a friendship. We can sit in judgment or feel judged ourselves by friends like these.

Conversely, it always benefits a friendship when we talk about our struggles and victories in the spiritual life. One of the greatest ways to build male friendships is to admit (confess) our sin. But spiritual superiority tends to be a defense mechanism that keeps people from closeness. When a couple of the disciples asked Christ, "Who is the greatest in the kingdom of heaven?" He called a child over to stand with them.

"Whoever humbles himself like this child is the greatest in the kingdom of heaven," He told them (Matthew 18:2–4). Children tend to talk about their problems and to see friends on a level equal to theirs.

Fear

Fear also keeps men from closeness with other men. Men who come from homes where dad was absent, abusive, or overinvolved create an unsafe atmosphere for friendships. They see other men as unfeeling and stoic and likely to reject them the way their fathers did. These fears cause them to doubt the value of trying to be open with friends.

There's a common fear, too, that other men will see us as needy or weak or will interpret our wanting a close friendship as meaning we are homosexual or have strong feminine tendencies.

The men I've counseled who struggle with homosexual feelings need close heterosexual male friends to find health. Many experts believe that men who struggle with homosexuality are really trying to have healthy, intimate friendships. Joe Dallas, writing to such men, states,

> To you, men perhaps seemed distant, unavailable, rejecting. Fear or resentment of them may have been a part of your response to that perception, and that response created an increased need for male love. When that need became sexual, you satisfied it through homosexuality. Then, when you realized that homosexual relationships were in conflict with your desire to please God, you gave them up. But you didn't give up the longings for men you had felt for so long. In fact, they have hopefully become stronger than ever.
>
> I say "hopefully" because those longings will motivate you to sustain the kind of relationships that will be a source of healing.[2]

Interestingly, the best way to deal with homosexual issues is through close male friendships. If you don't struggle with homosexual issues, close friendships will not lead you in that direction. Close male friendships actually enhance heterosexuality. If you do struggle with homosexual issues, realize that you can address those struggles without acting on such sexual desires. Those issues need not control you. (For a fuller discussion; I recommend *Desires in Conflict: Answering the Struggle for Sexual Identity*, by Joe Dallas [Harvest House].)

Women

Finally, women also stop men from being close. It's not that women try to keep men apart. Rather, it is men's fear of women that slows man-to-man relationships. Men in our culture tend to react to women in one of two ways. They are either passive or overcontrolling. Both reactions are based on fear. Thus you see men who spend all their time with their wives and family and shy away from close male friendships. Or they shy away from close relationships with their wives and spend all their time with "the boys." (Single men who are interested in one particular woman also may display one of these reactions.)

We need to strike a balance between these two extremes. Healthy marriages (and courtships) provide room for healthy friendships. And healthy friendships support growing marriages.

Men fear that their spouses will feel rejected if they develop close friends. And there are some women who fear they will lose their husband to his friends. But that fear can be dealt with through good communication and time commitment to the marriage. Men need to see that good friends promote a good marriage, that a break from life with a friend can enhance the marriage and rejuvenate a man's energy.

Men who ignore their wives at the expense of time with friends probably have superficial friendships. Men need friends to hold them accountable to spend quality time with their wives. They also need friends to discuss how to love their wives effectively.

Men have a tendency to expect their wives to meet all their emotional needs. This is part of that myth of the Hollywood Man—a perfect woman will bring total intimacy. This is a setup for affairs, as our wives' inevitable inability to be perfect for us leads us to go to another woman to talk about our problems. And that creates an emotional connection that can lead to an affair.

BUILDING MALE FRIENDSHIPS

Building strong friendships is a difficult task but something most men are willing to do. Friendships are like marriage—with work and attention, they will grow.

I met Pat at a typical business meeting. We had the common interest of rock climbing and had a similar background in youth ministry. We talked about rock climbing and about going together at some point. Eventually we set up a time. On the drive out, we talked about our pasts and what our lives revolved around in the present. We had a nice time.

After three more climbing experiences, the conversations were still at that level. I liked Pat but was hoping for more out of our friendship.

The Risk

After our fourth rock-climbing trip, I decided to take a risk. I had tried to be honest with Pat and shared some vulnerable stuff about myself. Now I asked Pat what he wanted from the friendship. I always feel like a weirdo asking such things, but that question began a depth of friendship that has continued to grow.

Pat was also willing to take a risk. He was hurting emotionally and was concerned how I would see him if I knew about his struggle. He was having serious marriage problems and was contemplating ending the marriage. I think he was afraid he would get judgment or unwanted advice from me, the marriage counselor.

I was just glad to have a friend. I could be a friend to Pat regardless of whether his marriage was falling apart. I think Pat would tell you that our friendship has had a big impact on his marriage. He has even told me our friendship came along at just the right time. He is now taking the problems in his marriage less seriously—they don't seem so terrible to him anymore—and enjoying the good parts of the relationship. As in this case, I truly believe a good friendship will help a marriage.

The risk is worth it. But my friendship with Pat worked out so well only because we have both committed ourselves to it.

The Commitment

Pat and I have a committment to spend time together. We still have great fun with each other, but the friendship has evolved into much more than just good times. We are committed to talking about our problems and our friendship. There's something humorous in two men telling each other they mean a great deal to each other.

Commitment and friendships don't always work out so well, however. Another friend, Joe, and I were starting to have some good times together. But I felt as though I did all the work in the relationship. I called him and set up times to get together. As we talked about our friendship, he said he wanted to grow closer as friends, but I never saw any action behind the words.

Eventually on a mountain bike ride we stopped to talk. I was honest and told him I wanted the friendship but that I would need him to initiate our times together. We had a long talk about the friendship. At the end of our conversation we decided to let it be up to him if he wanted to continue the friendship. I never heard back from him. He could not commit to the friendship. I still am hurt by this situation, yet I am glad that we are no longer playing a game.

Commitment in a friendship sounds strange, but it is essential both to having the time for the relationship to develop and to knowing the other person cares enough to spend the time with you. Without a discussion about the friendship the friendship will be superficial.[3]

Truth and Grace

Friendships need a foundation of both truth and grace. Christ's friendship with Peter is a good model for friendship. In Matthew 26 we see Christ relate with Peter. Christ is discussing His future and the death that awaited. Peter told Christ, "Even if all the other disciples lose faith, I will not." Peter is expressing his commitment. Christ gives him the truth, "This very night you will disown me three times." Even though Christ knows this when He goes to the garden, He takes Peter with Him. Christ shows grace to Peter, as He accepts Peter's flaws and remains his friend.

In the garden of Gethsemane Christ begins to be flooded with pain and emotion. Christ shares His deepest feelings with Peter, "I am in sorrow to the point of death." Before the night is over Peter will fall asleep as his friend prays and will disown his best friend three times. Now I don't know about you, but I might be ready to give up on this friendship.

After Christ's resurrection we see Him come to Peter again with grace. He has Peter "own" Him three times as He asks Peter the same question. "Do you love me more than these other men?" "Do you love me? and" Are you my friend?" (John 21). Peter replies yes to all three questions. Peter commits himself to the friendship. Christ gives Peter the truth and the grace to make that friendship possible.

Depending on your past (especially if you had an absentee, overinvolved, or abusive father), learning how to develop a male friendship can be difficult. For more encouragement and guidelines in developing friendships with men, I recommend reading *Bonds of Iron* by James Osterhaus, especially chapter 14, entitled "How to Begin."

The Value of a Friend

As noted earlier, having a male friend will aid your relationship with your wife and help your understanding of your father. Perhaps most important, a male friendship will help in understanding your sexuality. Friendships will give balance to your sexuality. There is something profoundly powerful when you have a friend who can relate to your sexual struggles. It is freeing. A close friend can hold you accountable. I don't mean telling each other how to act. Accountability is only valuable if you can really trust the person with real truth.

Accountability needs to be based on truth and grace. We need friends to ask us how we are doing with our thought life and hold us to the truth. We need friends to help us carry our burdens and have the freedom to confess our sins, without condemnation.

Finally, a male friendship meets our need to show love. Men need to love other men. I know that sounds scary. But we grow as Christians when we love other men. Men need to give other men affirmation and healthy affection. Giving a friend our time, feelings, and honesty is moving beyond ourselves. When we move beyond our own little worlds we develop the character of Christ in each other. I believe the closer we grow to friends the closer we grow to Christ.

TAKE ACTION

1. What keeps you from spending quality time with a friend? Do you find yourself struggling to communicate with your male friends? If so, why do you think the communication is difficult?

2. Who would you say is your close friend? Write his name down and contact him this week and thank him for the friendship you have developed.

3. Which friend do you have right now who might be worth the risk of discussing your sex life with? What

would stop you from taking the risk? If your friend told you a deep truth about how he was dealing with sex, how would you respond?

4. **Write a letter to your dad that you will not send and tell him all the good things he taught you about being a man. Then write about how you would have liked the relationship to have been different. Be sure to include in the letter what he taught you about friendships and male sexuality. Then read this letter to a close friend or your wife.**

8

THE SINGLE MAN

Tyler is forty-seven years old. He has just lost his wife after a grueling battle with cancer. He had been married twenty-six years. Now he's a widower and alone.

Jason is a nineteen-year-old college freshman. He grew up in a Christian home and is now attending a state university. He's amazed at the physical development that occurs between high-school girls and college women. He is a red-blooded American male and unmarried.

Jim is thirty-eight and just went through a bitter, two-year divorce battle. He has three young children, and after a fifteen-year marriage, he is single again.

Michael, a fifty-two-year-old factory foreman, has chosen to remain unmarried. He is a leader in his community and active in many important social concerns. Single and celibate, he's committed to the work of the church. All four men are single, sexual beings. Two of them have remained chaste; two have not. It's impossible today to stereotype singleness. It comes in many different forms. Everyone has his own story to tell. Whether one has been always single, sees himself as being temporarily single, or is single again, he has sexual struggles to face. This raises a series of questions for the single man. What is meaningful sexual expression? How does the single man deal with his frustration? How does he address his emotional needs that may lead to loneliness? How does he decide what to do with his sex drive in relationships? How does he go back to holding hands if he has experienced sexual intimacy in marriage?

There are answers to those questions, but finding practical solutions requires much thought, effort, and a willingness to face the pain necessary to mature. The struggle can also be very valuable as we understand our sexuality and what we have to offer in our current and future relationships.

THE FRUSTRATION OF BEING A MAN ALONE

In previous chapters, we've talked about how we're created to be in relationships with other people. We've also described the proper place of sexual intimacy in marriage. For single men there may be some—even much—sexual frustration in knowing the ultimate form of a sexual relationship, intercourse, is reserved for marriage. The Scriptures, though, are clear that sexual intercourse is reserved for the lifetime commitment of marriage. (The key passages are Matthew 15:18–20; 1 Corinthians 6:9–10; 7:1–2; 1 Thessalonians 4:3–7; and Hebrews 13:4.)

Still, every man must acknowledge and deal with the natural drive within him to connect in a sexual way with a woman. Our sexual drive does not mean we must have intercourse or even sexual encounters with women, but it means we must recognize our sexual desires and be able to express them in positive and healthy ways.

For those who have experienced a previous sexual relationship, the sexual drive is especially difficult to handle. Sometimes men who have been divorced seek sexual liaisons to express their sexual drives that seem to burn anew. I (Jim) have worked in therapy with many divorced singles who come out of an unsatisfactory relationship in marriage and begin to experiment with as many sexual partners as possible. These singles are quite often Christian men and women. Let's not kid ourselves—Christians don't always follow what the Bible says.

Clearly, that is a misuse of our sexuality. The desire to connect and be united with another person in only a sexual way promotes a kind of "I'll get mine" mentality. Ultimately what happens is a person ends up feeling guilty and either used or empty.

A certain amount of frustration is inevitable, but we need to take a good look at our thoughts and behaviors to see what we may be doing to promote excessive frustration. How are we spending our leisure time? What are we reading? What are we exposing ourselves to in terms of sexual literature or other media that encourage sexual expression?

All we may have to do is watch a lot of TV and we will experience sexual frustration, because most shows have some kind of sexual interaction. Sex is present in much advertising too, for sex still sells. If we expose ourselves repeatedly to situations fraught with sexual temptation, we will either yield and then experience guilt feelings, or we'll try to resist and increase our sexual frustration. We need to examine our thoughts and behaviors and find those things that may be promoting the frustration in order to begin to curb it.

HELP FROM ABOVE

A man may ask, "Does God care about my frustration? Can He help me to cope with my desire for intimacy?" The answer to both questions is a resounding yes. Let's briefly look at how both God the Father and God the Son help us deal with our sexual desires.

When we are experiencing sexual frustration and feeling a sense of deprivation, it's easy to cast God the Father as the ultimate "killjoy in the sky," the one who gives unreasonable rules to follow regarding our sexuality. In truth, that focus is all wrong. Remember, God created us with our sexuality both to worship Him and serve our fellow creatures. As the one who gave us our sexuality, He desires to give us guidance concerning our expression of it.

God has made it clear that sexual intercourse is intended for marriage. This rule is not intended to make us nuts; in fact, God desires that we use our minds to make sense of this command.

Our sexuality is meant to help me seek intimate relationships. His laws make sense. As David wrote in Psalm 19:7, "The law of the Lord is perfect, reviving the soul. The statutes of the Lord are trustworthy, making wise the simple." As our Father, God is perfect, loving, and just; His rules are based on the true and perfect love He embodies.

SEXUAL INSIGHT

A SINGLES' RENDEZVOUS

Singles bar, supermarket, laundrymat, or church? Many Christian men wonder where they can meet single women both for friendship and possible romance. In a mobile society in which people transfer jobs on average every four years and own one home less than seven years, it may seem that developing relationships is hard.

In spite of our cautions about the church contributing to the existence of the Church Man, we're happy to report that the church still remains one of the best places to meet and date a Chistian woman. The setting, in fact, can mimic that of a caring family, for churches have father figures and mother figures, and older and younger brothers and sisters in Christ. In such a setting, friendships can develop naturally, over time, as they do in the work and play settings of our lives.

The church can also begin to provide healthy socialization, especially as it moves to a better understanding of sexuality and of people relating as God intended. We encourage churches to look for opportunities to develop a welcome setting for single adults.

The church can provide opportunities for developing intimacy through both programs and people. Here are several programs various churches have used with success. Each offers encouragement and the opportunity to develop relationships with other unmarried men and women.

- Organized trips. That's a natural for a group of people who have time and energy to spend in social activity. Trips can be more than outings to the skate rink and bowling alley (though there's nothing wrong with those). A group can attend plays, concerts, and organize even bigger outings for discounts, such as boat crusies on a nearby lake or river.

- Bible studies. Many singles have biweekly or weekly studies at their church, or more often, in someone's home. In addition to studying a Bible book or an important topic based on the Scriptures, such studies often include refreshments and/or singing, and a time of prayer together. The studies often encourage discussion, and as people get to know each other better, an atmosphere of open sharing can take place.

- Service outreaches. There is a great sense of satisfaction in giving to others. Singles can be involved in many service projects that benefit others and allow them to interract in new settings. Christmas caroling at a nursing home, visiting an orphanage, helping program organizers by teaching in vacation Bible school, or volunteering as babysitters during a special church program are just some of the ways singles can be involved.

- Retreats and seminars. As social outings, these are special events because they have a distinctly Christian emphasis while they offer the fun of a new setting for play and interaction. A group of singles can rent a lodge for the weekend and hire a Christian speaker on the topic of their choice. Or they can attend a seminar or retreat already scheduled at a regional campground/retreat center and meet other singles in a learning and recreational setting.

- Recovery groups. Many churches offer divorce recovery groups and (for widows and parents who lose children) grief recovery groups or workshops. Such groups allow people to gradually take risks with one another without fear of judgment and criticism.

Remember, the purpose of church singles groups, like the purpose of any relationship, is not to "date and mate." It is to help each person to grow spiritually, socially, and emotionally. We encourage churches with many singles to consider how they may develop programs to meet the social and spiritual needs of single men and women.

Suggested Reading

Jerry Jones, *Single Adult Ministry* (Colorado Springs: NavPress, 1991).

Rick Stedman, *Pure Joy! The Positive Side of Single Sexuality* (Chicago: Moody, 1993)

He knows that it is in our best interests to draw close to Him. As we develop a fulfilling relationship with our Father, we are in a better position to move toward fulfilling relationships with others. When we recognize that sexual union is meant for a life-uniting relationship and not just immediate gratification, we can believe that God has our best interest at heart. He is preparing us for something better and lasting. As we recognize our sexuality as a gift from God and willingly submit it to Him, we can become content in following His guidance for our lives.

Jesus is a friend who has experienced temptations similar to ours; He can identify with us. And He has promised, "In the world you will have trouble. But take heart! I have overcome the world" (John 16:33). He has overcome all temptations—and, as the Son of God, even death—and is willing to help us.

How did Jesus resist all temptations? The Scriptures record that He often met with the Father in prayer, even rising before daybreak to visit with His Father (Mark 1:35; see also Luke 6:12). He found both His spiritual strength and intimacy needs met first in communion with the Father. Then he was able to have intimacy in close relationship with others.

Delayed Expectations

Another source of frustration for the single man comes not from sexual limits but a denial (or delay) of expectations. A man can so anticipate a relationship with a woman in the future that he quits living his life now.

Hank, age twenty-seven, essentially had put his life on hold. He had never married and had just completed a graduate school program. He was ready to begin living his life, but he felt he could not because he hadn't yet found the woman of his dreams. "Real life" was to have begun after high school, but then he couldn't start because of college. After college, romance was set aside again because of his decision to continue his education. After graduate school, he figured, his life would surely begin. But now his dreams were set aside again because life could not begin until he'd found the proper mate; only with her would he experience satisfaction and happiness. Hank continued to look to the next event in order to be happy. But putting off the enjoyment of his life in the present only added to his frustration and lack of fulfillment.

It's quite common and normal to experience frustration because of our desire for emotional involvement or attachment. Intimacy, closeness, and affection are all legitimate emotional needs, and they often seem only partly met for the single man. We may increase our chances for some of those needs to be met in our relationships with friends, in groups, at work, or in church, but, ultimately, we still look for that single significant other.

I believe God allows us to go through periods of singleness to prepare us not only for relationship, but also to learn to live a more significant Christian life. For those who never marry, singleness becomes an opportunity for career or personal development. For those who are divorced and thus single again, it becomes an opportunity to learn what went wrong in their previous relationship so as to not duplicate the mistakes in a new relationship. For those who are widowed, it becomes an opportunity to fully grieve the loss of a relationship before moving into another. If we don't take the opportunity to use our time of singleness for growth, we may misuse our sexuality out of frustration, and this will create a variety of problems.

Setting Boundaries

If you are single, you will be faced with the decision of what to do with that desire for sexual involvement. If you're alone and relatively uninvolved or unattached, it may not be such a big deal. But when you are developing a closer relationship with a woman, it becomes very important to know what you're going to do. As the relationship develops, at some point you probably will think about your deepening sexual feelings and may even want to have sex; as the relationship progresses, that desire probably will increase. At that point, you should have already made a conscious decision about how you will handle that desire.

Al and Debbie have been dating for about six months and are drawing closer to one another. They have worked hard to develop their relationship. They have faced and resolved some conflict, they've experienced some stress, and they've taken the time to get to know one another spiritually, emotionally, and intellectually. They've also spent time discussing each other's families and history. They've played together and worked together. It's not surprising that they're now beginning to experience sexual feelings toward one another.

They are both Christians, and they take their faith seriously. But they're also aware that the drive toward sexual intimacy is powerful. Both wonder how they should deal with their sexual feelings, so they discuss both their feelings and their choices.

One choice they quickly ruled out is to try to deny their sexual feelings. Al thought, *If we can ignore them, they'll go away, which will make our lives a lot easier.* But Al and Debbie soon realized that approach was ineffective in alleviating their sexual frustration. We commend Al and Debbie for their decision to not try this option. Choosing to deny your sexual feelings can make it difficult to rekindle them when it is time to do so in marriage.

Al and Debbie knew they needed to make an active choice because they had begun to set themselves up for involvement beyond their readiness. They found they couldn't deny their sexual feelings, and they hadn't really decided not to act on them. They didn't intend to be sexual with one another, yet they found they were putting themselves in situations that made the temptation nearly too much to bear. As they spent more time together, they became more physical. They decided to stop and analyze the options at that point.

Many people don't give themselves the chance to stop and think and move on ahead in what could be described as "innocent involvement."[1] They don't clearly draw the line, and as they get caught up in their passion, they move on to having sex. And consequences will follow, from sin and guilt to pregnancy, social diseases, and sometimes fractured relationships.

Al and Debbie had to decide whether they were ready to start behaving as if they were married. They had been doing some of the work necessary to develop intimacy in their relationship, which was preparing them for a move into total sexual involvement. They also were aware, however, that obedience to God, commitment, intimacy, and trust are all essential ingredients in a lasting, happy sexual life.

So they moved to the final option, which was to choose abstinence. This is the healthiest choice, as it's the biblical standard. But as mentioned before, that doesn't make it easy to carry out, especially as a relationship deepens. As Cliff and Joyce Penner note, "It is extremely difficult to choose to be a sexual person—aware of your feelings, knowing your impulses, responsive to kissing, touching, and caressing—and then choosing not to take your sexual desires to the natural conclusion."[2]

Al and Debbie found that in choosing abstinence, it was important to plan for their time together so they didn't set themselves up to test the limits. They were aware that Scripture doesn't talk about resisting temptation but commands us to "flee" it, heading in the other direction. They were also aware of their need to continue developing their relationship, and they tried to emphasize activities and settings that weren't so tempting. They found some value in reading Christian literature on the subject, such as Richard Foster's book *Money, Sex, and Power.*

Another choice Al and Debbie did not exercise was to accept a call to celibacy, as the apostle Paul did (1 Corinthians 7:8–9, 32–38). This is another option for single men and women—to live one's adult years unmarried and chaste.

Perhaps Al and Debbie felt God had not given them such a call. It is important to note the difference between choosing celibacy as a lifestyle and making a decision about abstinence. Celibacy is for those who feel called by God to stay single in order to serve humanity. They choose to channel their sexual energy into outlets of service.[3] Few people manage this well, but it is certainly one of the options. Every Christian, though, is expected to abstain from sexual immorality, which includes sex before marriage.

Those are the choices Al and Debbie faced and that all single people face as well. We must remember that with every choice we have responsibilities and consequences. We have to ask ourselves whether we're ready for the particular consequences of the choice we make. Choosing between the frustration associated with abstinence or the guilt associated with improper sexual involvement isn't easy. We need to make an informed decision, and we need help in order to gain the information needed for a wise decision.

GUIDELINES FOR INVOLVEMENT

It would seem that the decision on the level of sexual involvement for the single Christian man would be very clear cut. Doesn't the Bible just say "Don't"? The Church Man would offer a simple yes to that question, and he carries out any number of hiding strategies to keep himself from losing control. However, that is not always an edifying or practical approach; there are many levels of sexual involvement that I must decide about. The decision isn't just whether we're going to have sexual intercourse.

A fundamental starting place in making this decision is for the single man to get some sense of his values regarding proper sexual expression and limits. Part of this decision is understanding what may arouse you slightly or greatly. Men differ, of course, but we should never seek behaviors that make us vulnerable or make it difficult to abstain from intercourse. That's like stoking a steam locomotive with hot coals, starting the engine on a downward track, and then telling the brakeman, "Stop this thing at the next bend." It won't work.

To determine your values and set sexual standards, ask yourself the following questions: How do I feel about my body and sharing it with another? What are the boundaries that allow me to feel whole, safe, and protected from sin? What are my priorities?

The Bible provides the Christian's basic values. However, it is not really clear in terms of specific rules other than "Thou shall not commit adultery." Rather, other principles are developed in Scripture that we must try to apply to our personal sexuality. For example: "Love your neighbor as yourself." Ultimately, each of us has to make his own decision on how we demonstrate, or live out, such love. We each must decide; it won't work to have someone else decide for us.

With that in mind, here are several guidelines to remember about sexual involvement.[4]

Sex in Perspective

First, *keep sex in perspective.* We men are more than just sexual beings with distinct sex drives. God created each of us a whole person, someone with not only a body, but also a mind, emotions, a will, and a spirit. Sexual expression should include the involvement of every part of our personality. The man who sees himself as just an erect penis misses out on all the other dimensions of sexuality that God intended us to utilize.

Several Relationships

Second, *balance yourself with several relationships.* We need to be aware that as individuals, we have personal needs and feelings. Though we may want time alone and will need our own "space" at times, our needs and feelings often will find meaning in the context of a relationship with another person. Remember,

God created us to be in relationship with Him and others. Sexual expression is only one part of this. And just as artistic, emotional, and physical needs typically are expressed among others, so our sexual needs can be expressed among others, both men and women. We need to balance how we feel about ourselves with how we feel about a relationship. We need to balance our own sense of self-acceptance with a sense of mutuality.

Developing Intimacy

Third, think about the whole process by which you go about *developing intimacy.* Intimacy is a process, not a flip of the switch. It happens as an outgrowth of friendship, love, and commitment. This takes time and involves knowledge, risks, and certainly honest communication. It's also important to realize that there are many forms of intimacy besides sexual intimacy.

Howard Clinebell lists twelve different kinds of intimacy: emotional, intellectual, aesthetic, creative, recreational, work, crisis, conflict, commitment, spiritual, communication, and sexual. Although these are intertwined, research suggests that if 60 percent of them are met in the relationship, the friendship will have a better chance of being fulfilling.[5]

The healthy development of intimacy is foundational in any kind of positive sexual interaction. Intimacy begins with trust. We have the opportunity as men who are single to practice all forms of healthy intimacy and to develop ourselves so that if we should happen to marry at some point, we will be able to have a better sexual relationship.

Building Character

Fourth, consider how to *build character* in the relationship —your character. In our relationships we can learn patience, practice love and forgiveness, and show respect for ourselves and others. Relationships can give us opportunities to show honesty, to experience joy, and to have a childlike curiosity and playfulness. Cultivating those personal virtues will increase the likelihood of dynamic sexuality.

Singleness gives us the opportunity to learn the discipline of delaying gratification. Scott Peck defines this as "a process of scheduling the pain and pleasure of life in such a way as to enhance the pleasure by meeting and experiencing the pain first and getting it over with."[6] This discipline strengthens us by teaching us self-control, increasing our sense of self-worth, and helping us be less impulsive.

Learning Romance

A fifth area to consider is "Am I using my singleness as an opportunity to *learn the skills of romance?*" The ability to be romantic and a good lover extends well beyond one's physical endowment or knowledge of sexual technique. Reading the Song of Solomon, we see that the writer not only had skills, but also a healthy fantasy life. Romance involves learning to give and receive sexual pleasure.

Whether one is unattached, in a significant relationship, or married, the process of clarifying one's sexual beliefs and values is extremely important for the development of any current or future relationship. The divorced man needs to gain some understanding of why his marriage failed. Perhaps he never settled on a set of values before, but he must do so as a single person.

When We Blow It

As we proceed with the process of making decisions, we will surely make some mistakes. Wisdom is applying the knowledge learned from our failures. We will fail God and we will fail others, even though we don't want to fail. We fail because we are humans with emotional baggage living in a fallen world. We may fail in our relationships sexually or we may have one or more failed relationships. As such, we all have to grieve losses in order to grow and move on with our lives.

The losses can be especially acute for those of us who are divorced or widowed, because we acquire a special kind of emotional baggage as a result. If you are a widower, you not only must grieve the loss of someone dear who was part of your identity, but you are left with the "what if" regrets of things left unsaid or undone, of dreams and plans you now can only complete alone. If you are divorced, you may feel rejection or wonder whether you can love again; you may be bitter or self-condemning. No matter your emotional reaction after an ended relationship, remember that "God isn't finished with us yet." He continues to perfect and strengthen us for His service.

I know one minister and his wife who lost their southern California home one summer when torrid Santa Ana winds generated brush fires that engulfed their neighborhood. As the pastor and his wife were sifting through the rubble, they stumbled across a vase that had once rested on the fireplace mantle. As they rubbed the vase, the blackened soot and ash fell off. This couple discovered that while everything else in their home succumbed to the flames, this special vase remained intact. It survived because it had been through the fire previously at the glass factory, and it had been hardened and strengthened; the recent blaze could not harm it.

As a single man, God may be taking you through the fire and maturing you for a purpose, so that when a future trial may come in a relationship—or in your job or a specific spiritual service —you can say with the apostle James, "Perseverance must finish its work so that [I] may be mature and complete, not lacking anything" (1:4).

Whether your loss of relationship comes from widowhood, divorce, or the end of a long-term relationship, you can return to a sense of wholeness and completeness. Here are several guideposts in the journey to wholeness.

First, remember that making mistakes is part of life. You make mistakes just as surely as your wife or girlfriend made mistakes. As Paul describes it, "All have sinned and fall short of the glory of God" (Romans 3:23). Learning from mistakes is where wisdom begins. Continuing to try, even when we're discouraged and let down, is the kind of persistence James talks about in chapter 1 of his letter.

Winston Churchill defined success well as "going from failure to failure without loss of enthusiasm." The loss of a mate or a close woman friend will make us feel alone and even feel we are failures. And we may need to bear responsibility for our part of the loss. But in our failure we will learn much.

Second, remember that despite your feelings and doubt, God has good plans for you. During the loss of someone we love, our emotions are tender and that truth is difficult to understand. After I (Jim) once lost a significant relationship, a friend comforted me with a key verse, Jeremiah 29:11: "I know the plans I have for you, declares the Lord, plans to prosper you and keep you from harm, plans to give you hope and a future." I can now quote that verse without breaking into tears, but I must admit I recited it many times with a lump in my throat. I not only felt very alone, but I also felt scared, sad, and hurt.

During that period, God began to reveal the plans He did have for me. I started to learn more about what makes a relationship work and what doesn't. The beliefs about God that had been "head" knowledge and theoretical began to become much more real in my life. The hard work necessary to develop a relationship toward intimacy, to take the risk to rely on other men and women and to seek them out for support when I had been so ruggedly independent and self-sufficient, was just what God had in mind for me.

The important thing to keep in mind as we stumble along is that we are dealing with a process. It's important for the single man to live in the now, not just see life as something he's waiting for. Our now prepares us for the future. Our now will be more satisfying if we have learned from the past and recognize that God has us just where He wants us.

Third, have a healthy understanding of forgiveness. Forgiveness has been defined as "letting go of my need to hurt back when I get hurt." To release vindictiveness, we have to take ourselves out of the position of being the judge, whether that means judging others or judging ourselves.

Forgiveness is a spiritual process. As we see and accept the forgiveness we have from Jesus Christ, we're in a better position to learn to forgive others, as well as ourselves. Taking responsibility for our actions will also involve accepting the forgiveness that has been given us through Christ.

Unforgiveness will keep us stuck and ultimately will be emotionally and spiritually irresponsible. We need to forgive, make choices, accept the consequences for those choices, and continue to live and move on.

Finally, exhibit grace in your former and new relationships. God has and will show grace to you; so you show grace to others. The concept of grace was discussed in chapter 6. This is an essential truth to keep in mind as we try to cope with all our wrongdoing.

In making grace a part of our sexual experiences, consider the words of Lewis Smedes:

The discovery of grace is the discovery of creation's goodness as well as the discovery of sin's badness. It is the discovery that we can accept ourselves as sexual because our sexuality is one of the most exciting sides of the life that God created for us. Somehow, though we don't know how, our sexuality will be enhanced and glorified in God's perfect heavenly kingdom, just because it is the gift of God on earth. . . . Grace heals the distortions of sexuality so that the power of sexuality can come into its own.[7]

TAKE ACTION

1. Every man either is or has been a single man at some point in his life. Many men experience being "single again" as the result of being widowed or divorced. What frustrations do you experience as a single man (think of frustrations that are sexual *and* nonsexual in nature). How does your thought life contribute to your frustration? What behaviors contribute to your frustration? Remember that talking with a male friend may help, as well as talking to Jesus about your frustrations. Can you believe John 16:33 as a promise?

2. On a scale of 1 (none) to 10 (complete), how good are you at sexual self-control? How did you decide on that number?

3. What sexually tempting situations do you need especially to avoid? Be specific. How will you avoid them? What other people could you get support from?

4. If you've done anything in the past that makes you feel guilty, take time now to talk to God about that and experience His forgiveness and cleansing.

5. Review the issues regarding single sexuality discussed in this chapter, and make your own plan for where the boundaries in your relationships will be.

9

SEXUAL ADDICTION

Many men think they are sexual addicts because they think about sex so often. In truth, men tend to think about sex a great deal. Nearly all men dream about sex sometime in their lives. According to Weiss, 80 percent of males have sex dreams that result in ejaculation and more than 90 percent of men report masturbating.[1] So thinking and dreaming about sex is normal, and such thoughts are not always a form of lust.

Sexual addiction, however, is sex out of your control. It includes sexual thoughts that keep you from completing normal tasks during the day. Addiction may take the form of repeated self-stimulation, perhaps masturbating two times a day to relieve stress. It may manifest itself in visiting a pornography shop several times a year or visiting prostitutes regularly.

Sexual addiction is a behavior with severe consequences—job problems, loss of spouse, physical injury, financial problems, and/or spiritual problems. It can lead even to criminal activity, such as rape or child molestation. Even with such severe results, the addict continues to act out sexually. He is always trying to control or slow down his sexual behavior. He spends so much time thinking, planning, and acting out his sexual addiction that he ends up neglecting social, occupational, and recreational activities. He spends so much money on sex that he creates financial problems for himself. His addiction creates emotional barriers in his primary relationships.[2]

This chapter is for men who know those struggling with sexual addiction or suspect that at this moment they are trapped in the addiction.

Many men who are addicted don't know it or they deny it, much as those addicted to alcohol would deny their dependence. But when a man spends much time thinking or planning for his sexual expression, addiction is likely. When the time or money devoted to the planning or activity affects his relationships or job, he is probably addicted.

And the addiction can take one of many forms; it is not always a major criminal act such as rape, child molestation, or making obscene phone calls. Sexual addiction can include voyeurism, having sex with a consenting partner, or insisting your wife have sex two to three times a day. Some men express their addiction through vicarious sexual experiences and fantasies. The classic examples are voyeurism, exhibitionism, and indecent liberties. In voyeurism, a man looks into someone's house hoping to watch a woman undress; or he hangs around clothing stores trying to catch a glance of someone changing. In exhibitionism he wears clothing that leaves nothing to the imagination, little clothing, or actually exposes himself to others. In indecent liberties, the man touches someone in a sexual way that the person has not consented to or does not realize is happening. This takes place in elevators or other public places that make the act seem accidental. The addict may even apologize to cover his motive.[3]

Two Case Studies

Van is a sexual addict. He began to masturbate at age eleven and grew up in a home with very little physical affection and "no discussion of feelings and problems," he recalls. "My father never talked to me about sex. In fact, he seldom talked to me about anything except my grades and punishment. Mom was a very depressed woman and was physically sick a lot. So when I was hurting, I would escape into my world of masturbation. I would be able to sleep at night when I masturbated. I would wake up in the morning feeling guilty and ashamed of my behavior. I began to isolate from my family, and they didn't seem to notice."

During his high school years, Van was masturbating one to two times a day. "No one knew, but I felt like people could tell, so I kept to myself. I thought I was a pervert and feared I would never be able to have a relationship with a girl. I knew God was mad at me and somehow would punish me."

Van didn't use much pornography in his addiction; he used the fantasy of being loved. The thing Van wanted most was a close relationship; ironically, the addiction kept him from feeling anyone would ever understand him. He felt out of control, sinful, and depressed. He believed sex was ruining his life.

Alex is also a sexual addict. His addiction seems worse than Van's to the outsider, but the foundation and road to recovery are the same. Each needed to find the love and acceptance that God could provide; and, as we shall see, they needed to break the cycle of addiction. For Alex, the addiction has resulted in three marriages and hundreds of affairs. He is addicted to masturbation, pornography, prostitutes, topless bars, and affairs.

Like Van, Alex became addicted to masturbation while very young, when an adult male, in this case his uncle, did not portray male sexuality in a healthy manner. In fact, his uncle molested Alex at age nine.

"From that point on, I thought something was wrong with me. Why did my uncle choose me? Why did I let him do that? I never told anyone what happened to me until today," Alex revealed in one counseling session. "My uncle told me my parents would give me away if I ever said anything."

From masturbation, Alex moved to pornography in high school, then to topless bars and prostitution in college. "In my first marriage, the sex was never enough. I thought I deserved more, so I began having affairs."

As Van and Alex illustrate, addictive sex feels shameful. Often it is unlawful, stolen, or takes advantage of someone. Healthy sex, in contrast, creates a positive self-esteem. It has no victims. It brings more meaning to life and is based on honest, open communication.

Addictive sex compromises a man's values and morals. It uses fear to create excitement. Healthy sex, on the other hand, helps an individual accept responsibility for his needs. It uses feelings to create excitement.

Addictive sex is self-destructive and is used as a painkiller. But healthy sex is a decision two people agree on and is not used to run from one's problems.[4]

A Faulty Belief System

Van and Alex used sex in an addictive manner. Behind this addiction is a set of beliefs that give it power. Men like Van and Alex see themselves in ways that promote the addiction. These belief systems contribute to the addictive cycle.

Van would say it like this: "I know I'm a terrible person. I don't see how God could love someone like me. At times I hate myself and don't think I will ever make it in life." Van's belief that he is a bad person and that life will turn out badly gives him little incentive to try to overcome the problem.

Where does he find hope? Van explains: "What I am learning is that God does love me in spite of my sin. He wants me to grow out of my addiction and will help me do that. I am learning that I'm a sinner, but I'm also a person worthy of God's love."

Another belief system is found in Alex's words: "I never really thought my wife would love me for who I was and am. I worked hard to keep my addiction from her, knowing that if she found out, she would reject me. Inside, I believed no one would ever accept me for who I was. I was wrong. My addiction kept me from trusting people and allowing them to love me. When I did this, I just made the addiction stronger. My greatest need became sex. I believed I would die or have a total nervous breakdown if I stopped my sexual addiction."

This belief that sex is my greatest need is common for sexual addicts. Sex becomes their only coping mechanism to deal with life's pain. What makes this so powerful is that the addiction creates a great deal of their problems, yet sex is the only method they use to relieve their pain. It's a vicious cycle out of control.

Those beliefs lead to another one. Again in Van's words: "I can only trust myself to meet my needs. No one else can understand me or help me to make it through life." To counter this idea, the sexual addict needs to find people who will care for and understand him. Many attend group therapy sessions to find help and understanding; here men learn to allow other men to listen and respond. Another way to counter these faulty beliefs is to study and recall our valuable identity and worth as children of God and followers of Christ. As we look at Alex's story, we see how both group interaction and God's counsel can correct and redirect an addict's thoughts and behaviors, so that he is free to experience a healthy sexuality.

Finding Help From Others

Alex joined a group of men after his addiction had gone round and round in a cycle. Alex wasn't fully aware of the cycle; he only knew he couldn't stop, that he couldn't escape from sexual thoughts or activities. However, Alex soon realized that sexual addicts almost always are caught in a cycle that feeds on itself. Both the therapist and other men helped Alex recognize the cycle. After several sessions, Alex recognized his own cycle and explained it to us.

"In the beginning, the cycle was simple. I would have a problem at home or school, and I would begin to feel the pain. When I felt this way, I would begin to obsess on a girl in my class. I could spend hours thinking about her and living in a world of fantasy. This would take me away from my problems. These obsessive thoughts would move into a time of thinking about when and where I could masturbate. I would begin the planning stage for the acting out.

"Ten years later, the cycle is the same but more complex. I have a good or bad experience, and this experience runs through my beliefs about myself. If something good happens, I think I don't deserve it, but I want a reward. So I begin thinking about visiting a prostitute. I think about the last time and get lost in this world. When something bad happens, I go through the same thinking pattern to escape the pain. I leave reality to deal with reality. I seem to end up thinking about sex and don't even know why." This stage is called preoccupation.

Once Alex entered this preoccupation stage, he began his "ritual." Alex explained to the men his routine. "My ritual often begins by creating a fight with my wife. This can be about sex, money—just about anything. I leave angry and blame my wife for our problems. Deep inside, I think everything is my fault, but I avoid these feelings by blaming her. This sets up more preoccupation, and I begin to carry out my plans. Sometimes I feel like I'm in a trance; I'm a robot ready to act out. I come up with a reason to be gone from home or work for a couple of hours. I start cruising Main Street looking for a prostitute. I feel like I'm on drugs,

I'm high on adrenalin; the fear of getting caught makes the ritual even more powerful. Then I find a prostitute and have sex."

Afterward, though, Alex always was depressed. "I hate myself," he said to the group. "I ask for forgiveness, I tell myself I will never do it again. I begin to tell myself I'm no good, God hates me, not what I do, and no one would ever understand me. I often think about killing myself—everyone would be better off without me."

Alex was honest to us in his despair. He learned a lot about himself as he opened up to the other men. The power of a group of men meeting to deal with sexual addiction is noteworthy. Men learn how to communicate their emotions in healthy ways. Men like Alex and Van often are totally unaware what they are feeling until they begin talking with other men and listening to a therapist. A major reason men are unaware of their feelings is that early in life they were told by fathers and the culture that feelings were not valid or acceptable. As their feelings became stuck on the inside, the feelings actually control the person's behavior without his knowledge.

Men who are struggling with sexual addiction often blame those who love them for their feelings. This gives them the ability to rationalize their addiction. When they enter group therapy they generally hate the idea of being with other men and responding to a therapist. The power of caring and being cared for by other men, however, is life-changing. The ability to communicate feelings and not act on them is a major step in the healing process. As men find they are loved by other men and family, they often accept God's love for them as well. As men truly accept God's love, they often let other people in to love them.

Finding Help From God

Accepting God's love is a powerful force in a sexual addict's life, but it often is a difficult process. Most addicts struggle with believing that God loves them and often feel angry at God for not giving them a miraculous deliverance from their sexual addiction. Some believe they are too evil for God to love them and that He has given up on them. Like those addicted to alcohol or drugs, sexual addicts wonder whether God will continue to love them as He hates the sin they are involved in.

Yes, God hates sin, and addicts who fall back into a sinful behavior have a right to feel shame. But God does not abandon them. He has provided the means for restoration. The cure to spiritual addiction begins when a man realizes that God chose in Christ to forgive our sins. There is no sin God cannot forgive, and He will not give up on us if we fall back into sin. When we come to Him in repentence, He freely forgives (1 John 1:9). Each day is a chance for change and to let go of our past. He does not hold our trespasses above our head to show us how bad we are. Instead, we are told He "remembers your sins no more" (Isaiah 43:25).

Consider the strong words of the apostle Paul: "For I am convinced that neither death nor life, neither angels nor demons, neither the present nor the future, nor any powers [including sexual addiction] neither height nor depth, nor anything else in all creation, will be able to separate us from the love of God that is in Christ Jesus our Lord" (Romans 8:38–39).

Though God hates the sin of sexual addiction, He continues to love anyone through Christ who has this sin. By understanding and responding to this love, the sexual addict can receive words of love and hope, even as God calls the person into a lifestyle that brings wholeness in place of shame and despair. When we know God loves us and accepts us in spite of our sinful past, inner healing can continue and the power to transform both our wills and then our actions is available.

There is life beyond sexual addiction. No man is condemned to a life controlled by this addiction, and the more we accept God's unconditional love for us, the greater the ability to love ourselves and leave the bonds of this addiction.

We grow in our relationship with Christ and our ability to accept His love through study of the Scriptures (God's Word) and living through the Holy Spirit. Spending time alone and in deep fellowship with God are ways to experience the fullness of the Christian life. When we are very busy doing, we will not always hear God. Listening to God in silence will make it easier to recognize the lies we are telling ourselves. We can then do spiritual battle with those lies by believing the truth in God's Word.

CYCLES OF ADDICTION

Knowing God loved him in spite of his sin was a key step in Alex's recovery from addiction. The other was to recognize his addictive cycle and take steps to break through. Sexual addicts have seven stages in their addiction.

Stage One: Life Out of Control

Because of his lifestyle and often childhood problems that created an unhealthy coping mechanism, the sexual addict often finds his life is out of control. Once a man's life is out of control, he feels as if he is always messing up; he thinks he's making lots of mistakes and that people have it out for him.

In truth, his lifestyle is creating problems for him at home and work. His habit probably is bringing him physical, spiritual, and financial consequences. The only method he has learned to cope with these problems is the very thing that is creating the problems.

Stage Two: Feelings That Are Distant

Every man has feelings, and the sexual addict feels his highs and lows emotionally like everyone else. Typically for the sexual addict, though, the feelings are impossible to understand, and he may not even know what his exact feeling is at the moment.

Sexual addicts often grow up in homes where having feelings and expressing feelings are wrong. To feel sad is to feel weak, he learns. That falsehood is quickly accepted and eventually the addict learns to discount his emotions, often losing the ability to recognize his feelings. So when he hurts emotionally, he just feels bad but doesn't know why—he doesn't know that the emotion of depression or loneliness or loss is OK or even that it exists. Instead, he only knows in his hurt that he must relieve the pain, and sexually acting out is one way to relieve it.

Stage Three: Negative Thoughts

Not only is the addict unable to recognize how he feels, he does not realize what he is thinking on an hourly basis. But often daily he is telling himself negative things. In his head are the thought tapes, repeating themselves again and again. Tape 1 says, "You are terrible and no good. You're worthless." Tape 2 declares, "No one loves you. No one could ever love you if they knew what you really were. Even God can't love you."

Tapes 3 and 4 are no better. Tape 3: "Don't trust anyone to be there for you; God will not be there. Nobody can be trusted." Tape 4: "All you need is sex. Sex will relax you. You deserve a reward for all the pain you're in. Sex is the most important thing in life." Hearing these messages over and over, without others to correct his faulty thinking (a parent, a teacher, or a good friend), the addict begins to believe these messages as truth.

Stage Four: Obsessive Thoughts

The feelings and thoughts (stages two and three) set up the addict to become obsessed with thoughts of sex. He begins to think about sex to escape his problems; sex becomes a way to replace his pain with pleasure. In this stage the man can begin detailed planning of the sexual act, as well as engage in frequent sexual fantasies.

In this stage the addict can catch himself and go to God. He can ask God to show him the real source of his pain and ask for courage to face that pain. God meets us here. He does not condemn us for the pain; He feels the pain with us.

Stage Five: The Ritual

The addict begins to have a routine, often called a ritual. In this stage he may have thirty or even forty steps he routinely engages in, finally ending in his acting out his sexual desires. For instance, he may drive down a special road, stop by a minibank, visit a section in a bookstore, return home and pick a fight with his wife, then wear certain clothes.

All of this is preparation for his acting out. In performing the ritual each time, he feels anticipation and growing readiness, as well as a certain kind of "security" that things are the same. Then, when the ritual has been completed, he is ready to act.

Stage Six: Sexual Acting Out

Finally, after all the thoughts and feelings, the obsession, and the ritual, the addict acts out his sexual desires, engaging in some form of overt and addictive sexual behavior. It may be masturbation, occurring after the purchase of a pornographic magazine or while watching an erotic movie for twenty-five cents at a porno shop. It can be sex with a woman he picked up at a bar. The forms of expression are varied, but the outcome is always the same—despair.

Stage Seven: Despair

Once the addict has acted out his sexual desires, he feels shame, depression, guilt, and despair. Some addicts may even feel suicidal.

The addict does not have a healthy way to cope with his pain. He has no one to talk with about his problem. He feels guilty in asking God to forgive him again. Because he is unsure how to deal with his problems, the sexual addict lets his unhealthy thinking about himself and sex become cemented. Ironically, the results of his faulty feelings and thinking contribute to more faulty feelings and thinking, and the vicious cycle continues.

Once Alex understood his cycle, he realized he could not stop himself when he was cruising Main Street. He had to stop himself during the preoccupation stage and deal with the real problems in his life. He had to resolve the childhood abuse, and he had to feel the pain of his behavior in a safe setting and understand that God loved him in spite of his sin. Today Alex is no longer acting out his sexual addiction. In developing intimacy with men and his wife, he is healing his past.

When I said good-bye to Alex, I cried tears of joy and love. One of my greatest joys in life is to see men turn away from their sexual addiction and embrace love and acceptance from God, their wives, and other men.

The Healing Process

One of the first elements in the healing process is to fully understand the ritual and stop the addiction before it reaches stage six, the sexual acting out. Once a man is in the middle of the ritual, having followed a pattern of routine, the ability to stop the acting out is almost impossible. If, however, the sexual addict can understand the beginning steps of his ritual—driving by the bank when he has free time to pick up some "extra" cash, or stopping to browse in the X-rated section in the video store, for instance—he can act to cut off the ritual. Once he puts an end to the ritual, his chances of sexually acting out will slowly lessen.

Finding new ways to cope will need to replace the ritual, step by step. Activities like exercise, walking in a park, reading the

Scriptures and praying are all good methods of coping with sexual desires—and of coping with stresses of daily living.

Changing our feeling and thinking patterns is also very helpful in dealing with sexual addiction. Feeling patterns can be changed by meeting with a close friend to discuss the struggles of life. You will discover that your feelings are normal and that there are productive ways of dealing with them. Applying the truth of the Bible to how you see yourself will help with thinking patterns. Believing that God loves you unconditionally and wants to know you in an intimate way can dispel such thoughts as "No one loves me," "I'm a totally worthless person," and "God doesn't even care."

As indicated earlier in this chapter, individual and group counseling can be very helpful in dealing with sexual addiction. This could be a good place to start.

If you struggle with sexual addiction, there is hope. You will need help, however. That might come in the form of a close male friendship or your pastor—someone who can give you healthy accountability. It might come from the twelve-step group Sexaholics Anonymous. Reading the book *The Secret Sin* (Zondervan) by Mark Lasser can help. Or you might well benefit from seeing a professional Christian therapist who understands sexual addiction.

It takes a great deal of courage to ask for help, but I don't believe you can fix your own problems. The Bible is clear that we need each other to really live for Christ. And in our weaknesses, we can find true fellowship and love.

TAKE ACTION

1. During the next month monitor and evaluate your thought life, your habits in personal spending (any soft-core pornographic magazines?), and your sexual thoughts. At the end of the month ask yourself or discuss with a close friend how honest and healthy you are in the ways you deal with the sexual desires in your life.

2. **Has your sexual behavior or attitudes ever created problems at work, with finances, in your marriage, or in your spiritual life?**

3. **If you believe you are addicted to sex, who can you contact for help? It could be a friend, a pastor, or a professional counselor. If you are uncomfortable in seeking the help, why do you think you feel that way?**

10

SEXUAL DYSFUNCTION

Albert was on the verge of giving up. He was angry, depressed, and resentful. His marriage had been an emotional roller coaster for years, and now the coaster was at the bottom again. As Albert and his wife, Connie, sat in my office, they discussed how sex had become the battleground for their emotional war.

They still had some vestiges of love for each other and wanted to try to make their relationship work. But years of unfair fighting practices and tons of emotional baggage would have to be dealt with. As with many couples, the sexual relationship was a pretty good barometer of how the rest of the relationship was functioning. And Albert and Connie's sexual relationship had become a disaster.

As mentioned previously, sex is meant to be a celebration of the marital relationship. When the relationship is whole and healthy, sex will be great. We will have something to celebrate, and it will be a wonderful experience. When the relationship is troubled or dysfunctional in some way, however, that dysfunction will often be reflected in the couple's bedroom. Let's take a quick look at the sexual history of Albert and Connie.

Albert grew up in a very conservative, Christian environment, although it was probably more conservative and rigid than it was Christian. It seemed that when he was growing up, his parents viewed sex as evil or as the source of all evil. Albert still winces when he recounts the time when he was fourteen and his mother discovered him masturbating in the bathroom. He was given a tongue lashing, which created emotional wounds that still haven't completely healed. Neither parent offered Albert any formal sex education in the home other than a resounding "Don't." He was given the confusing message that "sex is dirty" and that you "save it for the one you love." There was little physical affection shown in his home. Albert's mother was a dominant, outspoken, controlling woman.

Albert had limited sexual experience prior to meeting Connie. He'd kissed a few girls and gone on a few dates, but he hadn't engaged in any major "making out" or had significant exposure to a female body. He had seen a few pictures of naked girls in magazines and was easily aroused by the young ladies he saw in school, but for the most part, Albert was sexually naïve.

Albert met Connie in his senior year of high school. They began dating and enjoyed each other's company. She was outgoing and friendly and treated Albert nicely. She had a strong personality and seemed at the time to allow Albert to draw on that strength and feel strong himself.

Connie was also the aggressor in their relationship sexually. Soon, with Albert's consent, they found themselves in the backseat of the car for his earliest sexual experiences; their activities were hurried there and also at his home, where they sometimes were sexually intimate before a parent returned home. So the pressure was always to hurry to get it over with before being discovered. Connie and Albert became good at stimulating one another through masturbation, and although they didn't have intercourse until shortly before they were married, risk, guilt, and shame had already become associated with their sexual activity.

Albert's Problem

What a surprise, then, that when they married in Albert's second year of college, when sex was finally "legal" between them, Albert began to have problems with premature ejaculation.

Albert found himself so excited when he was with Connie that sometimes he would ejaculate even before he entered her. Connie's response didn't help matters. She began to criticize him for "coming too quick." Though he tried to satisfy her anyway, it seemed that he could rarely do so, and she was quick to let him know her frustration.

To combat his problem, Albert tried thinking of other things to distract himself during intercourse. Thinking about work, baseball averages, and grocery lists did little to help, however, and it certainly did nothing for his own degree of satisfaction. So he tried tranquilizers and then even some type of anesthetic cream that was meant to minimize the sensation.

Nothing seemed to work. Instead, as he became more and more anxious about the sexual experience and began to focus more and more on his response, Albert began to find himself losing his erection as opposed to ejaculating quickly. This brought an entirely new wave of insults and criticisms from Connie. Now he had gone from "Quick Draw McGraw" to being "The Limp One."

Albert had not realized before what a temper Connie had when she didn't get what she wanted! This was the girl with whom he had had lots of fun. She had been a wonderful companion, and he certainly didn't want to displease her or, even worse, lose her. But as his pressure to perform increased, the hardness of his penis decreased. Connie continued to berate him for his sexual ineptness.

The trouble in the bedroom soon began to find its way outside as well. Without being aware of it, Albert was seething with resentment. Yet it was difficult for him to verbalize his anger directly to Connie. Instead, he questioned his own manhood and ability to perform. He needed a chance to feel like a success, so he put his energies into his business and then into church activities. (In case you hadn't already guessed it, Albert was also a Church Man.) This left less time and energy to invest in the marriage.

Obviously, if he was spending less time in the relationship, he was spending less and less energy in sexual activity, especially since the bedroom represented his primary arena for failure.

When Connie and Albert first came to my office, they had not had sex in four months. In fact, Albert held the belief that it just wasn't worth the effort and frustration. This set up the next line of attack from Connie. Albert was now referred to as "Mr.

Roper," an allusion to the character in a sexually charged television comedy; Roper avoided sex with his wife. Therapy was a last ditch-effort to save their marriage, because in addition to feeling sexual failure, Albert also feared getting a divorce. The problem was, he wasn't sure he wanted to live with Connie, either. Albert and Connie are a good example of a couple in the throes of sexual dysfunction. Not surprisingly, they are also a couple experiencing relational dysfunction.

Anger and Resentment— How to Kill Your Sex Drive

This chapter will look briefly at a few of the sexual dysfunctions that men may experience. Recognizing that men are to "keep the marriage bed undefiled" (Hebrews 13:4) and that the marriage relationship allows full expression of sexual love, this chapter is addressed specifically to married men, and in some discussions we will be appropriately specific. We will not go into detail regarding treatment, however, because there are many excellent resources already available that do that. Our goal is to help you recognize sexual dysfunctions and what may be causing them so you can seek the help necessary to resolve the problem as soon as possible.

Just as sexual addictions can be a result of uncontrolled obsessions, sexual dysfunctions can result from unaddressed repression. In chapter 4, we saw what happens to a relationship when we try to escape reality with our hiding strategies (defense mechanisms). Sexual dysfunctions can be a result of what happens when we fail to address those defenses and continue to hide from intimacy.

Unaddressed or unrecognized anger and resentment can be a major reason we utilize defenses. And although we may not always openly display our anger and blow up at our wife, there are many more subtle ways we can express our hostility. The bedroom provides a marvelous opportunity to express that stored emotion in a variety of ways. Don't get me wrong; I'm not trying to say that anger and resentment are the only reasons men experience sexual dysfunctions. Guilt, anxiety, depression, fatigue, and rejection all have their parts to play as well. But if we're angry and resentful toward our wife for whatever reason (and sometimes the reasons have even been created in the bedroom, as in the case of Albert), our sex drive will be affected. No man will want to go to bed with a woman who is as critical and "castrating" as Connie. We won't want to satisfy the woman who is fault-finding and rejecting.

Let's focus our attention on three of the most common sexual dysfunctions: premature ejaculation, impotence, and inhibited sexual desire.

PREMATURE EJACULATION

Like Albert, Steve found himself ejaculating within seconds of achieving an erection, and only rarely was he able to last long enough to even enter his wife.

Harry also was a premature ejaculator, or so it seemed. However, at times he thrust vigorously in intercourse for thirty to forty minutes. His wife was not orgasmic in intercourse and had no desire to become so; she preferred shorter couplings, and Harry concluded he needed to maintain the activity for an hour in order to bring her to climax. He believed the notion that more was better, that a few minutes longer might bring more enjoyment, orgasms, and even multiple orgasms. Thus he thought he was ejaculating too quickly, while his wife was actually getting tired of sex, thought his activity was taking too long, and was even becoming physically sore.

As you can see, *premature* is a relative term. Premature ejaculation is one of the most common sexual complaints among American men. The easiest definition is that the man arrives at ejaculation before he wishes to do so. It involves the lack of ability to consciously control when ejaculation of seminal fluid occurs. It should be noted that just thirty years ago, Kinsey reported that 75 percent of the men he interviewed ejaculated within two minutes of beginning intercourse. That was considered the norm at that time, and it didn't appear that Kinsey considered such occurrences to be premature. The real test of a good performance these days appears to be the ability to satisfy one's partner.[1]

That performance expectation is why premature ejaculation can cause resentment and frustration in sexual relations. "It is not uncommon for a woman to report that the man ejaculates prematurely eighty to one hundred percent of the time, whereas the man might report a ten to twenty percent occurrence. This difference in experience points out the need for clarification of the problem within the relationship."[2]

For men who have difficulty with premature ejaculation, the more they try to hold it off, the more it seems to speed up. All men want to have better voluntary control of their orgasm. The issue is not one of lasting longer but of what is happening to allow us to enjoy our sexual interaction. A man wants to have some control over his sexual response, whether he ejaculates after one minute or ten when in union with his wife.

Much of the obsession with lasting longer is due to how much culture exaggerates the importance of intercourse. Remember, intercourse is not the only sex that counts. There are many sexual activities that can bring enjoyment to both the man and the woman. And there is nothing particularly better to long-lasting sex versus the shorter kind.[3] Again, the main problem with premature ejaculation is that it generally does not give full satisfaction to the wife. So learning to exercise more voluntary control over our ejaculation is not only important for our own confidence as men, but also in terms of being able to provide more satisfaction to our wives.

There is no real consensus on what causes premature ejaculation. As in our example of Connie and Albert, a hurried pattern of lovemaking seems to be a common refrain. Ejaculatory control requires practice and an understanding and communication between a man and his spouse. But early sexual experiences in which the man hurried for risk of discovery often affect later performance. Men who have masturbated in the bathroom or have had sex in the backseat of a car may have inadvertently become conditioned to complete the sex act as quickly as possible.[4] Here is another reason to consider restraint as a single man. The solution to such previous sexual experiences is to retrain your attitude and associations about the process of sexual arousal.

Another common cause that seemed evident with Albert and Connie is conflicts regarding one's self or women in general. In some situations, a man may ejaculate quickly as a result of anger toward his spouse. In a passive-aggressive way, he achieves his own satisfaction and robs his wife of hers. This is quite selfish, but in a relationship fraught with conflict, it certainly wouldn't be unusual. In fact, researchers have shown that men who use sex that way may not even consider themselves inadequate lovers but may instead blame their wives for not being sexy enough.[5]

Recognizing and admitting that a problem exists is often half the battle won. Learning to slow down will help the man gain greater confidence in himself and will bring considerably more satisfaction to him and his wife. The answer is not generally to try to think about something else, take tranquilizers, or use some sort of numbing ointment, but rather to get to the place where he can feel more and experience the sexual excitement and sensation for as long as he likes. Many methods can help a man develop this ability, and they generally have one point in common: training the man to pay attention to his feelings of sexual excitement.[6] Whether he pays attention to the good feelings or knows when he is approaching ejaculation, he can take some simple steps to delay it.

It's essential for the husband to admit he has a problem with premature ejaculation. However, both he and his wife should see it as a couple-difficulty requiring cooperation to find a solution. I'm happy to report that the solution to premature ejaculation is really quite simple. A couple can easily learn various techniques and exercises that will improve ejaculatory control.

It is most effective when the husband and wife work together to address this problem and practice the exercises and procedures necessary to learn new techniques. There are many good resources available. I recommend Clifford and Joyce Penner's *The Gift of Sex* and Ed Wheat's book *Intended for Pleasure*, which provide a wealth of information and utilize a Christian approach.

IMPOTENCE

Impotence is the inability to achieve or keep an erection sufficient for intercourse. This is a tragic fear for most men, and even the possibility of looming impotence or waning sexual prowess will send many men to the doctor.

Impotence appears in all ages, all races, on every social level, and within every economic group. Helen Singer Kaplan asserts that approximately half of all men have experienced occasional times when they lost their erection or could not even get one for intercourse.[7] When a man experiences impotence, the vascular reflex mechanism fails to pump sufficient blood and hold it there to make the penis firm and keep it erect. It should be clarified that impotence does not refer to the inability to impregnate, which is sterility. Nor does it refer to the inability to ejaculate, which is called retarded ejaculation.

Impotence can take many different forms. Some men achieve no erection at all. Others get an erection, but as the love-play continues, anxiety sets in and the erection is lost. Still others may experience an erection that is maintained adequately up to the point of entry, but when entry is attempted, the erection dissipates. Then it's impotence if the man doesn't have the confidence or the relaxation to be able to let the erection return. In any extended lovemaking time, however, it's not uncommon for the intensity of the erection to wax and wane.[8]

In the majority of cases of impotence (more than 95 percent), the condition can be attributed to emotional factors that may have started in many different ways and have become perpetuated by a pattern of anxiety. Thus, impotence usually is caused by a man's thoughts. On rare occasions, it may be the result of a physical problem and not emotional distress. The easiest way to distinguish this is whether he experiences erections at anytime during the day or night. If he does, it is quite unlikely that the impotence is due to any physical cause. If he is never aware of erections occurring at any time, it would be advisable to undergo a physical and urological exam.

Most commonly, impotence is a result of some form of performance anxiety. A man may have an occasion in which an erection will not occur. The next opportunity for intercourse brings with it greater anxiety, which can be followed with more failure and then more anxiety, until a pattern of preoccupation and self-consciousness moves the man into what has been called a "spectator" role. When a man becomes a spectator regarding his own sexual experience, as opposed to a participant, he is less likely to experience sexual pleasure and the sensations necessary for arousal. Instead, he's attempting to take control of what is happening, and this preoccupation and demand he places on his body only makes the erection more difficult to attain.

In his mind, his fear is that he will not achieve arousal. It's as if I told you, "Don't think of the color green!" Now what's the first thing that pops into your mind? And often in reaction to an impotence experience, a man may come back and try even harder the next time in an attempt to prove his masculinity. Or the man may gradually lose interest in sexual activity and "turn off" to his wife, virtually trying to remove sex from his life.[9]

Recall our example of Albert and Connie at the beginning of this chapter. In response to ongoing demands and criticism from his wife, Albert placed great amounts of pressure on himself to perform. The more he focused on his inability to perform, the more difficult it became for him to either gain or maintain an erection. Connie's anger only increased the pressure on Albert and further inhibited his sexual freedom. His response became, "Why try—what's the use? The only thing sex is going to do is make me feel like more of a failure."

Impotence can get started in many different ways. It may involve, as with Albert, premature ejaculation, which creates anxiety about performing and moves the man to the "spectator" role. It can also be a result of drinking or drugs, especially since certain types of medication have that specific effect. It may be the result of dominant parents, particularly dominating mothers. A rigid home training where sex was viewed as evil can contribute. Impotence can also be a symptom of emotional depression. Or it can be a result of fatigue. In addition, a fear of rejection, guilt, other negative feelings, and any unusual stress can create impotence.

Any of the above causes may occur at any given time in one's life. The key is to not overreact when one's penis fails to cooperate. Anxiety and fear of ongoing failure create the real problem. When impotence accompanied by anxiety has occurred several times, it has a tendency to perpetuate itself.

The process of reversing impotence first involves taking the focus off the state of the man's penis and putting it back where it needs to be with intercourse—that is, on a total experience of love. A man will need to experience some form of distraction and do some refocusing. Second, he needs to have a partner who can positively enjoy his body. He will need to regain his confidence. The wife, too, will need to stop "trying" to bring about an erection.

The man will need to try to rid himself of his performance fears and the pressure that comes from the spectator role he assumes. Ed Wheat refers to a solution that involves three lines of approach: talking, that is, reestablishing the broken communication lines; touching, which refers to physical communication that may have broken down; and playful teasing, which suggests a kind of sexual relationship that can begin to develop even though the husband is still unable, or rather thinks he is unable, to gain an erection. Teasing involves spending time together and giving pleasure to each other without demand for intercourse; it is being playful rather than working at lovemaking.[10]

Talking is crucial. A couple must be willing to talk about either premature ejaculation or impotence with openness and honesty. It is essential that they talk about the man's sexual dysfunction, even though doing so may seem, at the time, like an extremely difficult challenge.

If a couple is having difficulty discussing this or has experienced years of impotence, they should seek professional help from a qualified counselor who has training with sexual disorders and understands how to help couples resolve conflicts and learn to work together again.

INHIBITED SEXUAL DESIRE

Milton grew up in a rigid sexual environment. He never received any sexual instruction from his parents. In fact, the instruction he did receive was that sex was evil and that one should not engage in it. He also heard severe warnings about the dangers of masturbation. Any kind of sexual interest or exploration on his part was dealt with critically and harshly.

Milton went to a boys' school through high school and was overprotected in that environment. He was what we might call a "Momma's boy." He finally married in his late twenties, having remained chaste until his wedding night.

Milton's wife initially came into therapy, frustrated because of her husband's apparent lack of interest in any form of sexual activity. He didn't like to kiss, and she referred to him as a "lousy kisser." He didn't know how to do anything in bed. He had read no books during his engagement or marriage, and had no discussion about his sexuality and sexual performance; he was fully sexually naïve.

Lawrence was a successful businessman. As a great initiator on business projects, he was viewed by his peers as quite a visionary. He was dedicated to his appointment book and was extremely organized in documenting his goals, objectives, and activities. He would accomplish a goal and move on.

Not surprisingly, he had approached the process of acquiring a wife in much the same fashion. It was a goal to be achieved. His young wife, Marla, fit the bill. She was attractive, intelligent, and confident. She was a good mother, and she could handle the social scene with great aplomb.

But Marla was becoming starved emotionally because her husband was rarely available to her and the family. Lawrence was a workaholic who invested little time in the relationship after the courtship was over. After he'd won Marla's hand, it was time to move on to the next project. Because he had little time and interest in the relationship, he also had little time or interest for sexual activity.

Whether one is sexually naïve or a goal-oriented, let's-get-down-to-business male, or he experiences serious emotional barriers, as Albert did with Connie, the result is often the same: a man who is not interested in sex.

Tensions or anxieties also can produce a lack of interest, including fear of pregnancy. So can a preoccupation with projects outside the family. I (Jim) was married eleven years before I had my first child, and I often joked that nothing served as a better method of birth control than a graduate-school education.

Inhibited sexual desire can also be a hiding strategy, as in Albert's case—a way to avoid intimacy, to use anger and resentment in a passive-aggressive way to escape pain and inflict "punishment." If this pattern describes you, it is essential for the sake of your relationship, and ultimately for the sake of your marriage, to have an open discussion with your spouse regarding how you feel and what might be getting in the way of your desire.

Kaplan's work on problems with sexual desire shows that unconscious barriers to feeling the need for or interest in sexual involvement often stem from the early childhood environment. And because of the strong impact of those early influencing factors, an individual is not likely to be able to resolve the problem without professional help.[11]

If the lack of desire is due to an identifiable stressor, however, it can often be addressed between the husband and wife. But most importantly, it is far easier to resolve a problem if it is identified before it becomes a full-blown dysfunction. Then the couple can begin to develop better forms of communication. They can take some time to learn about themselves sexually, to learn to give and receive pleasure, perhaps scheduling time together and planning for creativity and fun. They need to distract themselves from anxieties and demands and take responsibility for their own sexual response.

Addressing sexual dysfunctions will involve motivation, communication, and cooperation. Experiencing dysfunctions is like living in a home with a leaky roof. When it's raining outside (when the crisis occurs), the roof is leaking and we run around putting out all kinds of buckets to catch the dripping. It is exhausting, frustrating, irritating, and annoying. The next morning, however, it's sunny outside, and the last thing we want to do is address the leaky roof. We would rather go out and play. However, unless we get up on the roof and examine what kind of problems exist up there, we can be assured that when the next rain comes, we will be revisited by the drips and the drops, the frustrations and the irritations.

It's not easy to get up on the roof and evaluate the amount of damage. It might even be frightening to imagine what we'll encounter once we pull off the shingles and tar paper. But unless we do this and invest the energy necessary to face the problems, our relationship will never have a chance to grow as it was intended, and we will never achieve the depth of sexuality God desires for us.

TAKE ACTION

1. On a scale of 1 (lousy) to 10 (great), how would you rate your sex life? (Circle your response.)

   1 2 3 4 5 6 7 8 9 10

   What rating do you think your wife would give it? Why?

2. What problems, if any, exist in your sexual relationship?

3. List any fears you may have about sex. How can your mate alleviate those fears? Do you fully trust your mate with your body? If not, in what aspect? Why?

   Refer to 1 Corinthians 7:3–5, which emphasizes how one's body also belongs to his spouse. List any incorrect attitudes you may have about your body or your mate's body. Read Song of Songs 5:1–16 and 7:1–9, which describes our sexual attraction in marriage to our partner's body.

4. If you find that your interest in sex is diminished, consider the following questions:

Is there an obvious stressor in your life?

How do you feel when you are in a sexual situation with your wife? How do you feel when she initiates sex?

What do you believe to be your duties as a husband, lover, and Christian?

Discuss your feelings and beliefs with your wife.

5. Based on what you've read in this chapter, do you think you and your wife can resolve the problems yourselves, or do you need professional help? Why do you think that?

11

MAN TO CHILD

The sexual revolution that began in the late sixties has left its mark. If you're a father raising children or planning to have children, or if you have young brothers and sisters or nephews and nieces about to mature into men and women, the following findings may alarm you:

- Teenagers typically watch five hours of television a day, which means that in a year they have seen nearly fourteen thousand sexual encounters, according to the Center for Population Options.[1]
- By the time they are twenty, three quarters of young Americans have had sexual intercourse.[2]
- More than a third of fifteen-year-old boys have had sexual intercourse, as have 27 percent of fifteen-year-old girls, up from 19 percent in 1982. Among sexually active teenage girls, 61 percent have had multiple partners, up from 38 percent in 1971.[3]
- The onset of menstruation in girls has dropped three months each decade in recent years, so that urges that once hit at fourteen may now arrive at twelve. At the same time, the years of sexual maturity before marriage are much greater than a gener-

ation ago, as the typical age of a first marriage has jumped to twenty-five, up from twenty-one in the 1950s.[4]

- Eighty-five percent of the teenagers who have had sexual intercourse say it was unpremeditated the first time, and they were not protected.[5] Each year, more than one million teenagers, one out of ten of all women aged fifteen to nineteen, become pregnant. One in seven American teenagers contracts a sexually transmitted disease.[6]

WHERE ARE THE FATHERS

If you're a father like me, statistics like those scare you. Students are more sexually active than ever before, and they're also more confused. The purpose of this chapter is not to take another shot at fathers or go on about what a poor job fathers have done in preparing their children for the sexual pressures they will face. No, even though the statistics are frightening, we fathers can help our sons and daughters learn what healthy sexuality is about.

Hollywood appears to be winning the battle for the hearts and minds of our children. But we can't stick our heads in the sand and refuse to face the pressures our kids are confronting. Many of those pressures are the same ones we face in terms of coming to grips with our own sexuality and facing the temptations that exist around us every day.

Recently, I (Jim) have begun asking clients what kind of sexual education they received in the home and what part their fathers played in the process. Most clients report that they heard no discussion of sex in the home and nothing from the father. On occasion, a one-time sex talk may have occurred between father and son. I can only conclude that we men are either scared to approach the subject or uninformed and embarrassed with our lack of knowledge. Perhaps, instead, we are in complete denial, refusing to believe that our not providing information and not understanding the pressures our children are facing will have any future impact. That's not good enough! As fathers, we have the God-assigned job of providing a nurturing and protected atmosphere for our children.

In chapter 7, "Man to Man," we discussed four different types of fathers. I'd like to follow up on those as we begin to examine how we can nurture, support, and protect our sons and daughters.

Fathers, we have an opportunity to set the tone in the family with regard to how sexual subjects are discussed and displayed. We can jump in and participate in the character formation of our children. In fact, sex education is a process of deliberate character formation. But it seems most of us are confused about this process. Sure, we love our children, but when it comes to talking to them about a sexual subject or to dealing with teenagers period, we get flustered and hope they will learn their lessons elsewhere and not get hurt.

The behaviors and attitudes we learned in childhood often make it hard to achieve what we want the most when we grow up—to come close to other human beings. When we're children, it's appropriate to turn to our fathers for help. Unfortunately, too many of us did not get what we needed from them. So as adults, we're likely to continue to wish for others to fill our empty spaces. We believe our happiness depends on being accepted and loved. That makes it difficult for us to communicate important truths to our children. Yet their future sexual choices will be greatly affected by the overall quality of our relationships with them.

Fathers and Sons

Andy had an open and honest relationship with his father. The relationship wasn't perfect, as there were struggles, tough times, and disagreements. There were times when his dad admitted he was wrong, and there were times when Andy had to ask his father's forgiveness. But they had worked hard at it ever since Andy was a little boy. Andy's father was always there when he needed him. He wasn't pushy, he wasn't overinvolved, but he made time when Andy needed him. And through the years, he had instilled a solid core of biblical values in Andy's heart and mind. Andy felt free to discuss anything with his dad without fear of condemnation.

Andy was now sixteen and a sophomore in high school. Girls seemed to be blossoming all around him, and he couldn't help but notice as blouses, skirts, makeup, legs, lipstick, and perfume all challenged his senses. Andy was a fairly mature sixteen-year-old. He long ago had discussions with his father about sex and how God's purpose for sex is enjoyment in marriage. He had promised himself and his father that he would try to wait. Yet chastity was a whole lot easier at twelve or thirteen, when girls were far less appealing and his hormones were less demanding.

SEXUAL INSIGHT

SEXUAL EDUCATION

How we fathers discuss sexual subjects and sexuality provides opportunities to participate in the character formation of our children. In fact, sex education is a process of deliberate character formation.

But most of us seem confused about this process. When it comes to talking to our children about a sexual subject, we get flustered and hope they will learn their lessons and not get hurt. Some of us give a one-time "sex talk" and think that's it. But a loving father cares enough about his children to help them in an ongoing process of discussion and positive modeling.

Here are four key principles in sexual education emphasized by Stan and Brenna Jones in their book *How & When to Tell Your Kids About Sex*:

1. Parents are the principal sex educators; you will have either an anemic, unintentional, mixed-up impact or a powerful, clear, and positive impact.

2. The best teaching of a child occurs at "teachable moments" when discussion and instruction mesh naturally with the events of daily life. Parents should strive to become "askable" parents whom kids can come to with questions.

3. Positive messages are more potent than negative messages.

4. Repetition is critical; the most important messages about sexuality rarely "get through" on the first try.

You can help your child to make proper sexual choices when you establish positive channels of communication about his or her sexuality. As we provide our children with some understanding of their deepest needs, we will be able to help them make mature decisions as to how to have those needs met. We can help them learn to set boundaries, to be able to say no, and to be able to defend themselves.

This will all happen within an environment of a supportive relationship—one of love and encouragement.

Suggested Reading

Stanton and Brenna Jones *How & When to Tell Your Kids About Sex* (Colorado Springs: NavPress, 1993).

Clifford and Joyce Penner, *Sex Facts for the Family* (Dallas: Word, 1992).

His father had noticed Andy's increasing fascination with the opposite sex. One night after Andy had a date with a new girl, his dad dropped into his bedroom. "How'd it go with Diana, son?" he asked.

"OK, I guess."

"What is it? You've been checking her out for quite a while. Is something wrong?"

"Uh, I don't know. It's, uh . . . just that, uh . . . she gets me pretty excited."

"Is that a surprise?"

"Well, no, she's really beautiful. It's just that I didn't expect her to be so aggressive."

"Was she moving a little faster than you wanted?"

"Uh, kinda, and yet I can't believe my response. I mean, I had to tell her to stop, which wasn't really too fair, because I thought the girl was supposed to be the one to say no. Besides, I really wanted to keep going."

"It must have felt pretty good, didn't it, son?"

"Yeah, it did. But it just went too fast. Am I weird or something? I know a lot of guys would have gone all the way with her."

"What stopped you?"

"I like her, Dad, I really do. But I don't feel like I know her. But Dad, I wanted to have sex with her."

"That's a normal feeling, son. Anybody would have felt that in that situation. Do you know why you stopped?"

"Well, it would have been too easy, that's one thing. Two, I know it would have been wrong, but at the time I wasn't worried about that too much. Then I wanted to keep your trust. Also, I wanted to respect her. I think—I know this is weird—but I think I cared about her too much to do it. But most of all, I think I was just plain scared."

"How did she respond when you told her no, son?"

"I think she was surprised. Initially it seemed like maybe she was hurt, and then we talked about it a bit, and then I think she was thankful."

"What do you plan to do about Diana?"

"I'm not sure, Dad. I don't want to hurt her feelings, yet I'm not sure I'm ready for her."

"Son, I'm not sure she's ready for you. You did a very courageous thing tonight—and the right thing. I'm proud of you, and I know God is pleased too. You know, we talked several years ago about surrendering our sexuality to Jesus, and tonight you were accountable. I know it wasn't easy. As you said, a lot of guys couldn't have done what you did.

"It will probably be important for you to talk to Diana about what happened and why you did what you did. You'll need to discuss what kind of boundaries might be necessary for the two of you to feel safe with each other, because it seems like an awful lot of sexual energy and electricity gets generated."

"It sure does," Andy replied.

It may be difficult for you to imagine having a conversation with your father like Andy did with his. But it didn't just happen. It was a result of years of talking about feelings, about God's plan for our lives and sexuality, about sexual drives and energies, and about being honest and speaking the truth with love. It also came about because of the consistent example given by Andy's father toward Andy's mother. He sees his dad treat his mother in a kind and equitable manner. He sees him treat her with affection and respect.

Andy has also felt accepted by his father for who he is, not just what he does. The acceptance has to come first, so he feels free to act in a way that builds that trust further. As a result, Andy has remained accountable not only to his earthly father, but also to his heavenly Father.

Many of us learned about our sexuality shamefully, perhaps looking at a *Playboy* magazine or having rowdy conversations in the back of the school bus, instead of through a caring relationship with a godly father. Thus we grew up fearful of our sexuality and are unable to approach a woman without shame or thoughts of sin.[7] With shame comes a tendency to fear relationships and ultimately to avoid or withdraw from them.

One form of withdrawing is to exploit the opposite sex, to want to forfeit emotional and spiritual closeness and confuse it with sexual acts. Gordon Dalbey puts it this way: "The boy whose father talks to him openly and compassionately about the mystery of sexuality . . . need not protect himself behind harmful practices that enforce distance from the female. Indeed, such a father can affirm the wonder and mystery of his son's sexual energies, even as he holds the son accountable for expressing them in a godly way."[8]

In contrast to Andy, Danny has had seven different sexual partners. Five of the girls were virgins. He likes the attention and reactions he gets from girls. He has struggled with alcohol abuse and drugs, and he has had some brushes with the law. Formerly he was a B student, but this year he's having some trouble.

Danny likes sex. He describes himself as "addicted to flirting." He likes being with girls and says he can talk seriously with them. They listen and understand him better than guys. Danny has had a church upbringing, and his parents are professing Christians. He believes in God, too, but reacts negatively to the rigid life and stern God that his parents seem to impose on him. Nonetheless, he prays every night and before school in the morning.

Danny admits his parents have been permissive, and he sees himself as spoiled. He says he is scared to slow down, that calm is boring and he needs things that bring a rush. He likes risk, and he likes the excitement that comes with having sex. Danny is fifteen years old.

As we talked, it became clear that Danny's relationship with his father was essentially nonexistent. He desired to be with his father. He wanted contact with him, but they couldn't seem to connect, mainly because of his father's fear of his own son. Danny kept trying to get his dad's attention in so many ways, mostly negative and destructive. As a result of his sexual desire, he experienced repeated shame. With the shame came depression and the need to run away emotionally. He escaped into alcohol, drugs, and sex.

Yet there is still a soft side to Danny. He wants to be close, to have a relationship with a male who can help and understand him, who can give him a sense of strength and encouragement.

In therapy, Danny is just beginning to connect with his father and express his anger and frustration with his dad's distance, aloofness, and fears. It will be a long and winding road, but they may have turned the corner before it was too late. Fathers can connect with their sons, and the impact can be positive, even life changing in the attitudes and behaviors of their sons.

Fathers and Daughters

When Dennis came in for counseling, he was embarrassed because of how he was feeling toward his daughter. The feelings had even created conflict in his marriage and shame within himself. Dennis's daughter was fourteen years old, but her body was that of a well-developed young woman. She had "matured early," as they say. Dennis was now struggling with sexual feelings toward his own daughter. He was shocked, appalled, and disgusted with himself, and still he didn't know what to do about it.

Many men are surprised when they begin to sense ambivalent and even sexual feelings toward their daughters. They want to draw away. And that's how it was for Dennis. He and his daughter had always been close; she had always been "Daddy's girl." Now as she matured, he found himself beginning to pull away. He was afraid to wrestle with her or be too close to her, to touch her in the ways he had before. It seemed as if she wasn't his little girl anymore; she was becoming a woman, and that threatened him.

When Dennis first shared these feelings with his wife, she became angry and disgusted with him. She called him "perverted." Dennis too was beginning to question whether he was a pervert. However Dennis's feelings are not unusual. Many men experience a similar sort of response when their young girls start to become young women.

In therapy, Dennis was able to resolve the tensions with his wife that traced to several of her unmet emotional and physical needs. And he was able to end the continual withdrawal from his daughter.

Not all fathers will experience such feelings, of course. Yet dads need to be aware that as their daughters mature, as fathers they may have an alternating attraction/repulsion to their daughters. Typically this will happen in the mid teens, at a time when girls need the support—and even the touch—of their parents.

Unfortunately, at a time when both adolescent males and females need touch most, they seem to get it less from their fathers. At a time when this young woman especially needed ongoing love, acceptance, and support from her father so she would feel special and respected and worthy, Dennis was withdrawing out of fear of his own sexual feelings and arousal.

This can be incredibly damaging. Invariably, the daughter will then turn to other guys for the affection she needs, yet not feel worthy of it. And when she is removed from her father's protective touch and nurturing, she becomes fair game. If she is desperate, she might settle for mere sexual gratification or for being with someone who is not right for her, because she thinks she doesn't deserve better.

She will most likely make unrealistic demands on her partner as well. She may maintain a fantasy of being totally supported, protected, and valued. She may idealize her mate and become disappointed when he doesn't live up to her expectations. Disillusioned, she may have dreams of another man who will make her happy; those imaginings come from a deep wish to finally find a father figure who will love her. She may have difficulty trusting her beloved, doubt she is lovable, and continually seek reassurance or question her man's devotion. She will also have an exaggerated fear of abandonment and rejection. This will make her cling dependently to a partner or hold on to an unsatisfactory relationship far too long.[9]

We fathers must face our sexuality squarely and get a perspective on our needs, desires, feelings, and fears. When we do this, we're able to develop healthy relationships with our daughters and provide them with the help they need in cultivating their own sexual identity. We can help them develop their sexual identity in two ways. One is by modeling appropriate male behavior and attitudes in our relationships with our wives. This can give our daughters positive expectations for the male friends in their lives. The second is by supporting them with encouraging words and appropriate touches.

The Importance of Touch

Men can help their daughters as much as their sons by supporting them with words and touches. For both our sons and daughters, touching is essential to their growth and development. Family counselor Virginia Satir says, "People need four hugs daily just for survival, eight for maintenance. . . ."

Many men are uncomfortable with touching, thinking it unmanly or not knowing how, having not received it from their own fathers. But clasps to the shoulder, rubbing the head, giving hugs, and a variety of other touches can be wonderfully satisfying as expressions of personal caring and connection. Practice touches daily.

A few men also hesitate to touch their children because of fear of charges of child abuse or molestation. Again, appropriate touches, even in public, and your child's natural response will be to feel accepted. But what if you were abused, are sexually addicted, or are not sensitive about personal boundaries? Then it is reasonable that you pay particular attention to your feelings as you give and receive touch.

The Issue of Sexual Abuse

You may be uncertain about your own limits or the other person's when your children receive physical touch. Let any hint of unpleasant sensations be enough for you to stop the contact.[10]

One of the things that Dennis, the man in the preceding section, did *right* was to recognize and admit his feelings. This allowed him to discuss them and get the help needed to better his relationships with his wife and daughter. In many families today, the feelings are not admitted and discussed. Men who have been shamed themselves by abuse fail to form and maintain the boundaries that help keep the home environment safe and protective. When that happens, people's respect for privacy decreases, demands get made, exploitation and inappropriate teasing (either verbal or by touch) can occur, and others, especially children, may be taken advantage of for one's own emotional or sexual pleasure. That is sexual child abuse.

You may think that couldn't occur in a Christian home. But believe me, it can occur in any home where a person is not dealing with his sexual feelings in healthy ways.

The number-one predictor of child abuse is drug and alcohol abuse in the home, but a major contributing factor is a home with a rigid religious system. "It is difficult to measure one's Christianity, but researchers report that [sexually aggressive] adult males tend to be very devout, moralistic, and conservative in their religious beliefs," writes Richard Butman, a professor of psychology at Wheaton College.[11] Granted, there isn't always a real connection between religiosity and Christianity. But in homes that are closed off to the world, with a dad who is in charge to the extent that no one ever questions his authority, in homes where it's totally unacceptable to discuss anything about sex or sexual behavior, we have an environment ripe for sexual abuse. Oh, sure, it may not get to the extent that it involves incest (sexual intercourse), but sex abuse can occur long before we get into that type of behavior.

Remember, any time we begin using others for our own emotional or sexual pleasure, whether it be inappropriate teasing or touching, or fondling, we are exploiting or abusing them. And there are many closed family systems in the church—homes in which Dad may not have his act together sexually, homes in which father and mother may not be close and intimate and thereby modeling healthy sexuality for their children.

The consequences of such abuse are varied but always negative. After Donna suffered abuse by her stepfather from ages thirteen through seventeen, she was unable to recognize appropriate sexual boundaries in her relationship with boys. Without those boundaries she became sexually promiscuous. That's not at all uncommon. When boundaries are crossed through sexual abuse, the victim often will turn to sex in her desire to gain love and acceptance. Sadly, though other members of Donna's family suspected something wasn't right, they engaged in denial. Donna began a life of promiscuity.

Jenny demonstrated another common response to being sexually abused after experiencing inappropriate touching and fondling by a grandfather and an older brother. Her father was distant and aloof and did not provide her with the kind of protection and nurturance she needed.

Jenny began to develop a disgust and even a hatred for males. In high school, Jenny met a couple of older girls who seemed to take a special interest in her. They allowed her to share her feelings. They listened to her and accepted her. They provided her with nurturance, support, and encouragement. What also happened is they provided her an outlet for her sexual feelings and need for physical affection; she fell into lesbian relationships.

Through a series of lesbian relationships she at times felt safer, even loved and accepted. It was not because she had some great attraction for females; it was because of her intense fear and hatred of males.

Father as Teacher

An authentic man begins to understand his own sexuality. He is a loving father who cares enough about his children to help them in the process of learning about sex. I know this is scary, and I know most of us are not very good at it. But the time to start educating our children is during childhood. If we fathers don't take the initiative to begin this process, someone else will. Kids are picking up amazing information from the media, school, and their friends, and we need to be actively involved in giving them accurate, truthful, and biblical information.

I've interviewed dozens of clients, friends, and associates and asked what kind of sex education they received from their fathers. Almost without exception, every woman replied something like, "Nothing. He never said anything to me about sex."

For the males, the answer was nearly the same. The only difference was that some men had experienced at least a one-time sex talk. Yet there are many wonderful Christian resources to help us in the process. They provide information geared to children of different ages and help us parents know what's appropriate at various age levels. I recommend, for example, Clifford and Joyce Penner's book *Sex Facts for the Family* and Stan and Brenna Jones' book *How & When to Tell Your Kids About Sex.* The Joneses utilize twelve core principles of shaping your child's sexual character. (Four of those insights appear in the Sexual Insight earlier in this chapter.)

The process of sexual character formation will help our children meet their needs for relatedness and significance in healthy and godly ways. As we provide them with some understanding of their deepest needs, we'll also be able to help them make mature decisions about how to get those needs met. We'll help them develop their core beliefs about sexual morality and dating. We'll help them value the right things. Then we will have the opportunity to teach them the skills to handle themselves well, to set boundaries, to be able to say no, and to be able to defend themselves. This will all happen within an environment of a supportive relationship. We can provide them with a sense of strength at a time when others attempt to undermine their commitment to biblical morality.[12]

To get about the business of helping our children in this way, we must be able to look at our own attitudes and feelings about sexuality. If we're not comfortable with our own sexuality, we're going to have a difficult time helping our children understand their own. One way to assess this is to take a look at how our attitudes are played out in our own marriages. Are we able to talk about sex openly with each other? Many couples find this a difficult area to discuss without embarrassment, defensiveness, and hurt feelings.

The important point to remember is that we don't have to have all our own past baggage completely worked out and everything in place in order to do an effective job of parental sex education. If we're honest with ourselves about our defenses, attitudes, and blind spots, we can begin to do the job our own parents may not have done effectively. This will allow us to pass on a heritage of healthy sexual understanding and a confidence in the positive way God made us.

As we begin this process, we may find that many times we are learners along with our kids. That's OK, too. Being able to answer, "I don't know, but that's an important question, and I'll see if I can find out," is honest and presents a picture to our children that we are interested and sincere in our approach to the subject.

Let me encourage you to sit down with your spouse and evaluate the job you've done already in preparing your children. Then discuss your comfort level regarding sexual information or your own sexuality. As you are willing to endure some discomfort in order to build greater comfort, you will be on the road to knitting an environment of openness, honesty, love, and acceptance. You will be providing a foundation that can be built upon as your children grow and develop.

TAKE ACTION

1. On a scale of 1 (quite uncomfortable) to 10 (very comfortable), how comfortable do you feel about your own sexuality?

   1 2 3 4 5 6 7 8 9 10

2. On a scale of 1 (quite uncomfortable) to 10 (very comfortable), how comfortable do you feel discussing sexual matters with your children?

   1 2 3 4 5 6 7 8 9 10

3. Reflect back to your own childhood as to what you learned from your father about sex. Was the information gained complete, helpful, or basically nonexistent? What did you learn about sexuality from watching your father with your mother? With others?

4. As a father yourself, what have you decided to do the same way as your father in instructing your own children; what do you want to do differently? Have you already begun to apply these ideas in your home? If you have not, this is a good time to begin. Someone has rightly said, "The best inheritance a father can leave his children is a good example."

5. Evaluate your home in terms of the amount and kinds of touches that occur. Positive touches include hugs, kisses, handshakes, pats on the back, massages, sitting close, and letting a child sit on your lap; negative touches include shaking, pushing, slapping, and fondling your child. Ask yourself the following questions:
   (1) How many times a day do I touch others? Are the touches mainly positive or negative?
   (2) Do I touch some family members more than others? Do I touch some of my children more than others? If so, why?
   (3) Can I distinguish between safe and unsafe touch?
   (4) Ask these questions if you have one or more teenagers: Do I ever experience discomfort in touching my teenager? Do I ever avoid touching my teen? If so, why? Do I need to confess anything before my teenager and ask his or her forgiveness?

12

MAN TO WOMAN

Some recently seen bumper stickers:

"Women, you can't live with them, you can't live without them." "The more I learn about women, the more I like my truck." "My wife told me it's her or fishing. Boy, am I going to miss her."

I (Rick) see these bumper stickers frequently. Men don't understand women, and I must admit I can't figure women out. I love my wife, yet she is the very person I get most angry with. I desire to be really close to her, yet I'm afraid to let her see who I really am.

I was raised by women, and probably you were too. They were my mother, my teachers, and my baby-sitters. The majority of our childhood is spent being watched by women. Like most boys, in elementary school I teased the girls and hung with the boys. I believed that girls could give you bad germs but was willing to risk a game of tag.

As we begin to mature, though, our attitudes toward girls change. For me, girls became the focus of attention during junior high, those "Wonder Years." My friend and I spent hours talking about them. We had no idea how to relate to them, but we felt we had to have a girlfriend. We teased about how far we "had gone" with so and so, proving our masculinity. Girls became objects of desire, and I had posters of the latest model on my wall. I dreamed of sexual contact that would change my world.

In high school, girls started becoming "people," people I wanted to be close to; yet I was afraid of their power. They seemed to hold the key to my self-image and masculinity. I wanted them to want me without needing them. Somehow, I wanted to have the emotional power.

In college, I went from girlfriend to girlfriend. Seldom was I without a woman in my life. At times I was willing to sacrifice friendships with men to have a girlfriend. It was as if I needed a woman in my life to feel secure.

Later in college, I went through a period when I didn't want a woman in my life. I returned to an elementary-schoolboy view of women. As Christians, several male friends and I had a "bachelors till the rapture" club. Underneath this facade of individualism, however, I wanted a partner, a woman to really love me. You can see the push and pull of the need for a woman in my life. Women were real and I was confused. Perhaps your encounters with women have been equally confusing in those teenage and early adult years.

Seven years later I got engaged—I was in love! I had found the perfect woman for me. She was a goddess; I couldn't see her flaws, and she couldn't see mine. She was a spiritual, athletic, and sensual woman. That time in our life was great fun, filled with romance, laughter, and sexual desire.

Yet I too believed our sex life would be like the movies: I would please her for hours, and she would never get enough. Our marriage would be different from those around us. We would live without struggle and conflict. If we did have problems, our love would overcome them.

Then we got married. Our honeymoon was not your typical Hollywood romance. The pressure to have great sex created problems. My wife, Karen, wanted to spend time enjoying the sights and the relationship—sex was not her main priority.

Six months into the marriage, I thought Karen was becoming my mother. I felt she was too emotional and needed help. She seemed to make me do things I didn't want to do; I felt I was being manipulated. The sexual relationship was not so smooth, either. We did not know how to make sex a really positive experience. She did not seem turned on by me and my body. I felt obsessed with sex and thought it should be a daily occurrence.

Once again, I was confused by the opposite sex. Who in the world are the females? How can a man figure them out?

ALMOST ALL ABOUT WOMEN

My wife is like most women. She lives in a different world from mine. In marriage counseling, I like to shock people by saying, "My wife is married to someone besides me and has different children than I do." I actually mean it. Our wives do not see us the way we see ourselves, nor do they hear what we think we have said. They don't see our children the way we do. They don't feel the way we do about marriage generally or about our marriage in particular. The more we try to convince them that our world is the "right" one, the farther they move away from us.

On the positive side, we will never totally figure our wives out. If you are single, you will never be able to understand your lady before marriage. If you wait to figure her out, you will never marry. And if you marry her thinking you know her, you are in for a big shock. When we become husbands, there is always more to learn about our wives, because women change and grow. As husbands, we will have the privilege to be part of that change. The marriage will go through different stages, and we will continue to learn about women.

HOW WOMEN SEE SEX

Herb and Nancy sought marriage counseling after they had been growing apart for five years. As their children moved into junior high and high school, Nancy had gone back to work. During the past three years, her career had taken off. She began to make more money than Herb and develop new friendships. Herb tried to be supportive, but deep down inside, he found Nancy's success threatening.

Herb recalled, "I began to feel distant in the marriage. I felt like I was second place in Nancy's life. As I backed away from discussing these feelings, Nancy seemed to back away sexually. This created more confusion for me. I began to doubt her faithfulness to me.

"I had been frustrated for years in our sexual relationship. I just lived with the frustration, hoping somehow Nancy would figure it out. Now I'm angry and cannot handle her cool rejection of me."

SEXUAL INSIGHT

MEN VS. WOMEN

Men and women *are* different. The two sexes regard sex in distinctive ways; often the way one regards a sexual issue is the direct opposite of the other. Men often assume women will regard sex the way men do and have similar feelings. For instance, as the movies and TV portray women often as having an aggressive sexual appetite and approach, so the Hollywood Man (described in chapter 2) assumes this is how women are: they are hungry for sex and expect him to be aggressive and a master in his sexual performance.

Ironically, the truth will alleviate the pressure many men feel to perform sexually. Most women do not regard sexual performance or even the sex act as foremost in the sexual relationship. Women tend to connect sex with the overall intimacy in the relationship. They will feel sexual and be highly aroused when they sense their husbands are honest, caring, and close to them as individuals. At times the contrast is stunning: men can think that sex is a way to solve intimacy problems, while women find it difficult to be interested sexually if there are relational problems. This can lead to many problems in marriage.

Here are a few of the most important differences between how men and women view sex and respond in a sexual environment.

Arousal. Men tend to be aroused quickly. Many men can achieve an erection without much foreplay. Their imagination can quickly stimulate their bodies. In contrast, women thrive on much touching and being held; soft words and closeness begin to arouse their bodies. Women respond to a gentle and gradual touch as their bodies warm and prepare for the man.

Men also are highly sensitive to what they see. Men are often turned on by the sight; a woman much less so. While a man can respond quickly to seeing part of his wife's body or a certain piece of lingerie, a woman is turned on by feeling close in the relationship, sensing a man's care and protection. In addition, a woman is aroused more often by touch than sight.

The Role of Sex. Men tend to believe that sex is very important to their marriage and their life. They regard sexual intimacy, especially sexual intercourse, as important expressions of communication and affection. In contrast, women tend to place sexual relations lower in importance to the marriage, after communication, showing affection, romance, and safety. Most women want quality and quantity time together and resolution of relationship problems before they can enjoy sex.[1]

The Act of Sex. Men tend to be initiators in their sex lives. The good news is women are more likely to be the responders, so this is a good fit. However, this tendency creates some tensions. A woman may be interested in sex but because she wants the man to initiate, she will rarely do so herself; she may drop clues but she feels the man should be the strong, "romantic" one by initiating. In addition, most men like women to initiate at times. A husband finds the woman's interest flattering to his ego and feels masculine when a woman seems to "want him." Because most wives will only occasionally initiate, husbands can feel unattractive and frustrated. Even when they ask a woman to "make the first move" more often, they will find women still will wait on the husband much more than initiate the proceedings.

Discussing sexual problems. Women are not afraid to talk about sexual problems, nor are they highly concerned with sexual performance. Men, however,tend to be performance-oriented; when it comes to sexual performance, they often regard any problems as their fault. As men we tie our masculinity to our sexual ability, so discussing sexual problems hits us where it hurts—our masculine identity. Yet open communication is the only way to fully deal with sexual problems. Women tend to value working through such problems and do not relate masculinity to a man's sexual performance; that truth should help men to open up in conversation.

Suggested Reading

Willard F. Harvey, Jr., *His Needs, Her Needs* (Grand Rapids, Mich.: Baker/Revell, 1986).

Bernie Zilbergeld, *The New Male Sexuality* (New York: Bantam, 1992).

During the counseling process, the issue of sex became a focus. Herb reported, "In the past, Nancy never really seemed interested in sex. I always did the initiation. She didn't seem to understand my needs, and I thought she was just less sexual than most women. I wanted her to see sex the way I did. Sex was a way we could feel love. I wanted her to think about sex and make sexual advances to me."

Nancy did not agree with Herb's view of their sex life. She and the majority of women see sexuality very differently from men. For her, sex was less important than the relationship. She wanted sex to be good but was much more concerned about being understood and resolving the conflict in the relationship.

"I don't understand how you could be interested in sex right after a fight," Nancy told Herb. "When we're having problems and you don't want to talk about them and resolve them, I lose all my interest in sex. Today you act as if our problems are sexual. I think we're not talking about our problems, and you seem to avoid me." She wanted Herb to understand that affection outside the bedroom was more important to her than the sex itself.

Herb was surprised to learn that Nancy had been giving signals about sex and her desire, although she didn't feel comfortable initiating the actual sexual experience. She would try to set the mood by initiating touch and conversation long before entering the bedroom. She also wanted Herb to know that when he rolled over and fell asleep after intercourse, she felt used and unloved.

Nancy explained, "I am much more concerned about the process and follow-up than I am about the sex act. For me, sex is not just intercourse. Sex is relationship. I'm not turned on by the thought of sex or seeing Herb in the buff. I am turned on by the times he would listen to me and give me a feeling of closeness."

Like Herb, many men are learning to see women differently. We're learning that they cannot meet all our emotional needs. We're learning that men need to be intimate with God and other men to get some needs met. That women see sex differently. That men are visually oriented and women are relationally and emotionally oriented, although men also want the relationship to be growing and close. We are also realizing that women struggle with healthy communication just like us.

THE ROLES MEN PLAY

Though men should play the roles of boyfriend or husband to their girlfriends or wives, often they play different, negative roles. In our relationships with women we need to understand the roles we can fall into. If we do, we can make positive changes to our relationships. The four roles I will describe are common in marriage and as examples concern husbands, but an unmarried man who has dated one woman for a long time can also begin to play one of these roles. If he can recognize his role while single and begin working on it then, he may make such roles less likely to dominate the relationship and a future marriage.

When we assume any of these roles, we are not taking a healthy position as equal partner in the relationship. We are moving in front of or behind the woman, instead of beside her, as God intended.

At different times we can play different roles in the relationship. We will benefit our wives (or if single, our girlfriends) and ourselves if we leave these roles to become the husband or male friend we should be.

The Father Role

Lee was the oldest of five children. His father was a surgeon who had a highly successful practice. His mother raised the kids and was involved in volunteer organizations. Lee, being the oldest child, was given a great deal of responsibility for the other children. His mother used guilt to get Lee to help out. Lee would hear messages like these: "A good son would help his mother out. . . . Your father is never around, and raising you kids is killing me. . . . Without you, I don't think I could make it." Consequently, Lee felt a responsibility to be an emotional support to his mom.

While dating, Lee did not always exhibit his tendency to be a father figure; signs were there, but neither Lee nor his girlfriend, Beth, noticed. When Lee married Beth, he assumed in earnest a role similar to the one he played at home. He was more like a father to Beth than a partner. He reported, "I felt responsible for Beth's emotions and any problems we had. If we had an argument, I would make peace as quickly as possible. I took the blame for our struggles and tried to come up with good advice and solutions to our problems."

Because Lee was playing the father role, he seldom discussed his feelings and needs. He was so afraid of asking Beth about their sexual relationship that he never touched the subject. "I believed that if I loved Beth in the right way, she would met my needs sexually," he said. "I even felt guilty about wanting more sex and thought I was just a selfish person. I thought that having sex once a month should be enough for me."

What this father role actually created was emotional distance. Beth told Lee, "I actually want to know you and what you're going through. At times, I want you to be a father figure for me. I find myself becoming dependent on you." For the relationship to develop real closeness, both Lee and Beth would have to change the roles they were playing.

The Boy Role

Tim was raised in a home where Mom was always taking care of his problems. In junior high, he was having problems in English class. The teacher gave him some F's on assignments he failed to turn in on time. When his mother found out about the problem, she went to the teacher, covered for Tim, and got the teacher to give him another chance. That next week, Tim's mom basically wrote the papers for him. This pattern repeated itself throughout Tim's life.

When Tim got in a relationship with Jan, he repeated the pattern. He often waited for Jan to call and depended on her to make the decisions about what they would do, what they would eat, and what they should talk about.

In the sexual relationship, Tim left the decision in Jan's hands about how far they would go. Meanwhile, he would complain that Jan didn't love him if she wanted to spend time with her friends. He even got her to clean his apartment—she couldn't stand the mess and would end up cleaning for him.

Tim did not have outside friendships and ended up waiting for Jan. He was emotionally dependent on her. He even hinted that if Jan left him, he could not go on living.

If Tim and Jan were to get married, we might find Tim struggling to keep a job while Jan provided for them. Jan could end up working forty hours a week and coming home to take care of Tim emotionally and physically. In their sexual relationship, Tim would end up complaining about Jan's lack of love. He would use sex as a way to feel cared for and demand that Jan meet his every need. You can imagine the sexual problems this could create.

Tim and Jan would have some major changes to make regarding their roles. Tim would need to learn to be responsible in many areas, and Jan would need to let him fail. They were ready to commit to marriage, and these unhealthy roles had to change. Tim would need to learn to be assertive. He would need to no longer ask for permission to do the things he wanted. He would have to let Jan go and have a life outside their marriage.

The Teenager Role

The teenager role is one I see many men play in their marriages. They often agree with their spouses to prevent conflict. But then, while they're doing the very thing they agreed to do, they make it a miserable time. They go along with the authorities, but behind the scenes, they rebel. These men are often passive-aggressive in their relationships.

This was my favorite role early in my marriage. My wife would say, "Let's go to the mall and do some shopping." My tendency was to answer yes to any of her requests. So we would go to the mall. But while we were there, I would make the experience unpleasant. I wasn't doing this on purpose; it just became a role I was used to playing.

In our sexual relationship, I might initiate sex, and if I got turned down, watch out! I would say, "That's OK, no big deal." Then I would not help out with the chores or the kids. I would be passive, not sharing my real feelings and hurt. Then I would be aggressive, making Karen pay for letting me down. As I write this, I realize how immature it sounds, but during those experiences I wasn't aware of what I was actually doing.

I often work with clients who use this role to legitimize their sexual acting out, pornography, masturbation, and prostitution.

The Dominator Role

Victor was raised in a culture where men acted as if they were in control of their women. He watched his mother be totally controlled by his father in an argument. Once Dad was out of the home, however, he knew who actually ran the show—Mom.

Not in Victor's marriage, though—he wore the pants in his home. He would not allow his wife to work outside the home. He chose their house, their friends, and her friends. He told his wife when he wanted sex and how he wanted it. Victor eventually realized, "I tried to control every area of my wife's life. In reality, I was emotionally and physically abusive. Our sex life was more like prostitution than love. My wife even faked orgasm to avoid any kind of verbal whipping.

"In actuality, I was afraid of my wife. You would never believe it from the outside, but I thought the only way to keep her was to force her to be submissive. If I was gentle and kind, I thought she would leave me."

The reason Victor's wife stayed with him was her own abusive father. She believed Victor would change. She also believed somehow that she deserved his mistreatment.

Even for Victor, the sexual relationship was unfulfilling. "Deep down inside, I wanted to be loving and intimate," he says. "It was not too late to change the roles. I could become a partner, not a dominator. In this process of change, I got in touch with my feelings and began to break down, to ask for forgiveness and to let go. As I discussed my fears, I became less abusive." In the dominator role, a man tries to take control. He doesn't find satisfaction, however, for intimacy escapes him and his wife is unable to express her opinions and thus help her husband.

In all four of these roles, a core feeling of fear is common. Fear of rejection. Fear of being controlled. Fear of honesty and conflict. Fear of hurting the other person. Fear of being known. Fear of failing.

WHY DID I PICK HER?

The majority of us pick our spouses because they fit our patterns. In our courtships we are attracted to women who seem to offer what we lack; they fit into the puzzle and seem to complete our pattern. In a way, that's great; a man should marry someone who will meet his deepest needs. But the trouble is we think the woman will know what those needs are, even though we do not tell her and sometimes we are not certain ourselves what they are.

Having picked her, how do you make your relationship grow? *If you choose to understand what those needs are and learn to communicate them, the marriage relationship will grow.*

The ways we try to get our needs met are seen in our patterns. The romantic feelings during the courtship and early months of marriage are based on our patterns fitting with that special woman. Let's look at the case of Stan and Kate to see how these patterns work.

Stan says, "I came from a home where the problems were clear. My father was an alcoholic. I remember times when Dad would come home drunk and fall asleep in front of the TV. My father was not physically abusive; he would just pass out. Mom was the person who would take care of the problems. She would cover for my dad at work and with friends. Our family never discussed the problems. There were three unwritten rules in the home. One, don't feel; two, don't talk about the problems or your feelings; three, don't trust people."

Kate says, "I grew up in a Christian home. My father was an elder in the church and a successful businessman. Mom was a very religious person. They spent a lot of time with the family. Problems in the family were not talked about, and they worked hard to keep their children in line. I respected my father but never felt close to him. When I wanted to talk to Mom about problems, I would get a sermon. I felt like having a problem or negative feelings was a lack of faith."

Stan and Kate both did well in school, where they met and fell in love. When they married, they brought their families into their marriage. The patterns of relationship in their homes reproduced themselves in the marriage. People often told them they did not understand how they ended up together, coming from such different backgrounds.

Kate married Stan because he was such a hard worker, like her father, and because she felt acceptance for who she was, not for her performance. Stan married Kate because she was a sensitive, caring person. He believed she could understand him as he was. As Stan explains, "The very reason we married was that we gave each other what we did not get in childhood."

The early part of their relationship seemed perfect. They seldom had problems, and when they did, they tried hard to work them out. The early relationship was so romantic because they were meeting each other's needs without having to discuss them." Two years into our marriage, the family patterns began to create problems.

"I found I was no longer comfortable talking about my feelings and felt misunderstood," Stan said. This was what childhood felt like. Kate felt like I was always giving her advice and playing a hero and father role in her life."

As the two of them started looking at how their parents communicated with each other and with them, they began to understand how their upbringing affected their marriage. In discussing their own needs, they realized that what they didn't receive from their parents during childhood, they were now trying to get from each other.

Stan needed to talk about his feelings and find acceptance. Yet he found it difficult to trust others, including his wife. Thus Stan had no idea how to ask for the very thing he wanted . Kate also wanted to be loved for who she was, not for how well she performed. She didn't know how to accept love that was not based on performance.

Once this couple recognized their needs, they talked about them and began working to meet those needs for each other. At first it was difficult to really understand what the other was saying. Stan and Kate were having to change the patterns of communication and risk asking for their needs to be met.

Interestingly, this difficult journey benefited their sexual life. They began to talk about how to give each other affection that was both sexual and nonsexual. Their communication helped each other to see the other person as a child needing unconditional love. They stopped mind reading and began listening in a whole new way. They didn't blame their parents for their problems but chose to understand how their parents affected their relationship.

PSYCHO-BABBLE?

I know that many men find this psychological stuff about childhood hard to swallow. We would like to think we can choose our reactions to our wives without childhood problems getting in the way. I spent the first three years of marriage thinking that way. Our marriage was good in most respects. We could have made it without understanding our patterns from childhood.

The benefit of understanding those patterns, however, was amazing. I began to see my wife in a whole new way. I also found that what I thought she was thinking was much more my view of women than the reality of who she was. For instance, I planned to go rock climbing one Saturday with a friend, and I had already asked for permission to go. Karen gave me the OK. On my way out the door, she asked what time I would be back. Now, I grew up in a home where you tried to guess the right time so as to not disappoint or create an argument. So I thought about the absolute earliest time I would make it back and told my wife that time. In retrospect, there was no way I would make it back at that time.

When I came home two hours late, Karen was upset. When she expressed her anger, I got angry back. Who did she think she was, telling me when I needed to be home?

We had been working on our communication, however, so we put it to work. She told me she grew up in a home where Dad did whatever he pleased. He was inconsistent in his behavior. We discussed this problem for about an hour, listening to each other's point of view. Eventually the whole focus changed. I realized that what was important to my wife was a realistic guess about when I would be home. She didn't want me trying to make her feel good about letting me go by giving her an overly optimistic estimate. She wanted consistency. She did not want to be my parent, telling me when to be home. I had to change my view of her and see her as a partner, not a parent. By discussing how time issues were worked out in our childhoods, we found that we were expecting each other to respond the way our parents responded. Without our discussion, we would have run into this problem over and over.

This kind of struggle in communication develops real closeness in a relationship. Without such effort, our intimacy would slowly decay and the sex life will not be as fulfilling.

Developing Sexual Intimacy

Eight steps to a better sex life? These are not guarantees to sexual bliss, but I really believe that if you work on the following steps in your marriage, you will find a fulfilling sex life—not perfect, for we are, after all, sinners who will fall again, but fulfilling. If you are single, many of these steps will help you improve the relationship with the woman you care for. Following these suggestions cannot only help your girlfriend and you know one another better, they can deepen your friendship and help you evaluate any ideas about marriage.

Step one: Focus on the relationship, not on the sex. In fact, if you're a single man, focusing on developing a relationship often will lead to romance. Many men who began relationships that focused primarily on friendships later fell in love with the woman they had grown to cherish as a friend first. If you are married, focusing more on developing the relationship with your wife will contribute to sex becoming a strong, healthy aspect of the relationship.

Good sex is a symptom of a good marriage. Sit down tonight and ask your wife how she sees your relationship. Is your marriage what she thought it would be? What did she think marriage would be like? In the future, how would she like the marriage to look?

Step two: Practice listening. I spend most of my day listening to people. When I go home, I forget how to listen. My tendency is to solve my wife's problems long before I really know what she's saying. She's the most difficult person in my life to really listen to. Why is that? Because I am emotionally connected to her. What she feels, I often feel responsible for. When I realized Karen did not want me to help, I was confused. But what she wanted was for me to understand.

Whether you are a married or single man, you will learn more about the woman in your life by practicing reflective listening. This type of listening requires that you reflect to your wife or girlfriend what you understand her to say. Such listening will both clarify meaning and help to resolve (and prevent) misunderstanding.

When Karen and I first started to do reflective listening, we had to put it on paper and repeat back what we heard. We also had to put every sentence in the form of an "I" statement.

Reflective listening looks like this:

Karen: "I feel like you would rather spend time with your friends than with me."

Rick: "You feel like I would rather spend time with my friends than with you."

Reflective listening does not look like this:

Karen: "I feel like you would rather spend time with your friends than with me."

Rick: "Well, that's not true. I want to spend time with you." Besides being defensive, such a response does not give you time to think upon the statement nor accept it as the way she perceives things.

Whatever your spouse tells you about how she sees the world is true for her. Remember, in her perspective she is not married to you, has different children than you do, and does not see the world the way you do. When you practice reflective listening, avoid giving advice, avoid making sure your point is correct, and act as if this person is telling you this for the first time. If she thinks something is a problem, don't try to tell her it's not. Before you can ever come up with a solution to a problem, you must understand the real issues going on. There's a tendency to move to problem solving too soon.

Step three: If you're married, set up a weekly or biweekly date night. You don't have to do the typical evening date. My wife and I have enjoyed breakfast dates, lunch dates, and dates after the kids have gone to bed. We often cook a late dinner together. The focus of these date nights is an assessment of the status of the relationship and resolution of everyday problems. Of course, you can use these times to practice reflective listening .

Step four: Start or continue to do things that make your wife feel loved. (This and the subsequent steps are specifically for married men.) Have your wife make a list of specific positive behaviors that you are currently doing or have done in the past. Have her make a list of ten things you could be doing to increase the romantic feelings in your marriage. Make a list of ten things your wife can do for you that meet your needs. For example, "Let me know you respect me and what I do. Fill my cup with coffee in the morning." Be positive and specific, not vague like "Let me know you care."

Step five: Talk about your sex life. Even for men who have been married for years, this can be an awkward thing to do. Without a discussion about how their sex life is going, however, husbands may not understand their mates' needs. Men need to find out what their wives like or dislike about sex. I find it best to talk about our sex life at a comfortable time. This means a time other than right before or right after, which is the worst time if things are not going well.

It's also important to talk during the sexual act to make sure your wife is comfortable with your actions. As difficult as it is, you need to ask if what you're doing feels good to her. Just because a certain touching feels good to you does not automatically mean it feels good to your wife. Find out what pleases your wife most in the foreplay and what helps bring her to orgasm.

Communicate to your mate about what you like and what your dreams are sexually. Don't be afraid to introduce some creative ideas, but make sure your wife is at ease with your plans.

Talk about your fears as well. As Cliff and Joyce Penner have written,

> Sexual issues are important, so important that they must be talked about in detail. God intended for men and women to have sexual fulfillment in marriage. The only way for you to gain this fulfillment is to share your anxieties and difficulties. In order to build positive sexual self-esteem and establish new sexual patterns, you must first understand your old patterns and perceptions. And you must be clear in describing how you each have experienced your sexual interaction."[2]

Step six: Get educated. Men tend to think sex should come naturally. But knowing how the female anatomy works is a key to a good sex life. Men also need to know that women's arousal is a much slower process than their own. (See the Sexual Insight in this chapter.)

Through reading, you can recognize many of the myths that men tend to believe. Here are seven common ones, passed to us through Hollywood, friends, and our own faulty thinking:

Myth 1: Older men lose their sexual desire.
Myth 2: Men want sex all the time.
Myth 3: Men have affairs for the sex.
Myth 4: Men understand what women want sexually.
Myth 5: Men are comfortable talking about sex.
Myth 6: Men should not have sexual problems.
Myth 7: Men are responsible for their wives' orgasm.

Two books on sexual technique I recommend to husbands are *The Gift of Sex* and *Restoring the Pleasure*, both by Clifford and Joyce Penner.

Step seven: Re-create the romance. Put some thought and creativity into the nights you decide to have sexual relations. I find many couples do much better if they set up the time beforehand and make the whole evening a quality time. If you begin the night with some good communication about life, the chances of an enjoyable sexual experience increase.

Think too about the atmosphere of your bedroom. Make it safe from interruptions such as children, phone calls, and TV. Be sure the lighting is comfortable for your wife—stay away from the doctor's-office feeling. I suggest candlelight as often as possible. Spend some money on the furnishings too and be prepared with birth control material so as to avoid interruptions.

We can contribute to the romantic mood by looking and smelling our best. Brush your teeth, take a shower, and shave. My wife finds kissing me disgusting when my stubble creates a rash on her face. I keep an electric razor on hand for our special nights. Also, give your wife a chance to take a bath. This will often relax her and make the sexual encounter more pleasurable.

Step eight: Slow down. Making sex a rush job creates an atmosphere of "get it over with so I can go to sleep." See the sexual experience as involving the conversation, foreplay, intercourse, orgasm, and afterplay. Try to make sex less goal-oriented and more relational. Remember, your wife is made to enjoy a gentle, gradual process as part of her arousal for intercourse.

The movie *Sleepless in Seattle* depicts the dream many men and women have: find the right person and life will work. Certainly it's worth pursuing the woman you are in love with, but there is never the perfect woman. The reality is we will feel we have the perfect person one hour and two hours later doubt if the relationship will ever work.

Ultimately, women cannot bring true happiness to life. They are human beings with their own baggage just like you and me. But marriage is the place where we get the greatest chance to work at human love. We must choose to make love happen. Sex is a result of hard work on the relationship. It has its rewards, but great marriages don't just happen. With effort and perseverance, however, they are possible.

TAKE ACTION

1. Go through the four roles listed: father, boy, teenager, and dominator. Ask your wife (or girlfriend if single) which role you tend to play. Find out how she sees you playing that role. Remember that you may not be aware of the role you play.

2. Talk to your wife or fiancée about your childhood. Try to remember how Mom and Dad communicated. What was their pattern? Was it safe to talk about anger? Were you allowed to disagree, have your own opinion? Whom did you talk to about problems in your home? Why that person? What did you always tell yourself about "When I have kids, I will . . . "? What do you wish you would have received from Dad as a child and adolescent? From Mom? Then listen as your wife or fiancée does the same exercise; listen closely.

   Ask your mate how she sees your family. What kind of patterns does she see between your father and mother? How does she see your relationship with your mom? Remember to use reflective listening on this one; it could get uncomfortable.

3. Make a date with your wife or girlfriend in which the goal will be to make, discuss, and give to each other a list titled "Ten simple things you could do to make me feel more loved and appreciated."

NOTES

Chapter 2: The Hollywood Man

1. Michael Medved, *Hollywood vs. America* (New York: HarperCollins, 1992), 108.
2. Landon Y. Jones, *Great Expectation* (New York: Coward, McCann, & Geoghegan, 1980), 59–60.
3. Bernie Zilbergeld, *The New Male Sexuality* (New York: Bantam, 1992), 520–21.
4. Christopher Lasch, *The Culture of Narcissism* (New York: W. W. Norton, 1978), 199–200.
5. Michael Medved, *Hollywood vs. America*, 107–8.
6. Tom W. Smith, "American Sexual Behaviors: Trends, Sociodemographic Differences, and Risk Behavior," a paper presented at the American Enterprise Institute, Washington, D.C., 18 October 1993. Smith was reporting results of the annual survey of the NORC, which measures social attitudes and behaviors to determine social trends in America. See also "Study: 15% of Spouses Cheat," *Chicago Sun-Times*, 18 October 1993, 1.
7. "News Watch," *Washington Watch*, 29 October 1993, 2.
8. Rick Ghent, *Five Myths of Male Sexuality*, (Chicago: Moody, 1994), 25.
9. George Barna, *The Future of the American Family* (Chicago: Moody, 1993), 68.
10. William Masters, Virginia Johnson, and Robert Kol, *Sex and Human Loving* (Boston: Little, Brown, 1986), 337.
11. Daniel Evan Weiss, *The Great Divide* (New York: Poseidon, 1991), 68.

Chapter 3: The Church Man

1. Lewis B. Smedes, *Sex for Christians* (Grand Rapids, Mich.: Eerdmans, 1976), 51.
2. Jerry Kirk, "Christianity and Good Sex" in *Pornography: A Human Tragedy*, edited by Tom Minnery (Wheaton, Ill.: Tyndale, 1987), 60.
3. As quoted in Smedes, *Sex for Christians*, 17.
4. Kirk, "Christianity and Good Sex," 60.
5. Leland Ryken, "Were the Puritans Right About Sex?" *Christianity Today*, 7 April 1978, 13–18.
6. Clifford and Joyce Penner, *Sex Facts for the Family* (Dallas: Word, 1992), 161–62.
7. Stanton L. and Brenna L. Jones, *How & When to Tell Your Kids About Sex* (Colorado Springs: NavPress, 1993). Several of the ideas in this chapter about sex education at the different ages were drawn from subjects in the Jones' book.

Chapter 4: Men in Hiding

1. Dennis Coon, *Introduction to Psychology* (St. Paul, Minn.: West Publishing, 1977), 334.
2. Frank B. Minirth and Paul D. Meier, "Personality Types and How to Cope," videotape (Richardson, Tex.: Christian Family Video, 1991).
3. Coon, *Psychology*, 342.
4. Ibid., 335.
5. Clifford and Joyce Penner, *Sex Facts for the Family* (Dallas: Word, 1992), 191–92.
6. P. Cameron *et al.*, "Cognitive Functionings of College Students in a General Psychology Class," a paper presented at the American Psychological Association convention, San Francisco, September 1968, as reported in Coon, *Psychology*, 337.
7. Ibid., 338.
8. Ibid., 338–39.
9. Ibid., 340–41.

Chapter 6: The Spiritual Man

1. Gary J. Oliver, *Real Men Have Feelings Too* (Chicago: Moody, 1993), 264.
2. Lewis B. Smedes, *Sex for Christians* (Grand Rapids, Mich.: Eerdmans, 1976), 32.
3. Brennan Manning, *The Ragamuffin Gospel* (Portland, Ore.: Multnomah, 1990), 14, 26.

Chapter 7: Man to Man

1. Gary Oliver, *Real Men Have Feelings Too* (Chicago: Moody, 1993), 25.
2. Joe Dallas, *Desires in Conflict* (Eugene, Ore.: Harvest House, 1991), 159.

3. For further discussion of the importance of commitment and communication for effective friendships with male friends, see James Osterhaus, *Bonds of Iron* (Chicago: Moody, 1993), chapters 4 and 6.

Chapter 8: The Single Man

1. Clifford and Joyce *Penner, Sex Facts for the Family* (Dallas: Word, 1992), 192.
2. Penner, *Sex Facts for the Family*, 194.
3. Ibid., 195.
4. Douglas E. P. Rosenau, "Sexuality and the Single Person," *Journal of Psychology and Christianity*, 1: (Winter 1982), 30.
5. Howard J. and Charlotte H. Clinebell, *The Intimate Marriage* (New York: Harper & Row, 1970), 29–31.
6. M. Scott Peck, *The Road Less Traveled* (New York: Simon & Schuster, 1978), 19.
7. Lewis B. Smedes, *Sex for Christians* (Grand Rapids, Mich.: Eerdmans, 1976), 105.

Chapter 9: Sexual Addiction

1. Daniel Evan Weiss, *The Great Divide* (New York: Poseidon, 1991), 76, 82.
2. Patrick Carnes, *Don't Call It Love* (New York: Bantam, 1991), 11–28.
3. Mark Lasser, *The Secret Sin* (Grand Rapids: Zondervan, 1992), 33–34.
4. Ibid., 254.

Chapter 10: Sexual Dysfunctions

1. Bernie Zilbergeld, *Male Sexuality* (New York: Bantam, 1978), 255.
2. Clifford and Joyce Penner, *The Gift of Sex* (Waco, Tex.: Word, 1981), 269.
3. Zilbergeld, *Male Sexuality*, 258.
4. Ibid., 259.
5. Ed and Gaye Wheat, *Intended for Pleasure* (Old Tappan, N.J.: Revell, 1977), 86.
6. Zilbergeld, *Male Sexuality*, 261.
7. Wheat, *Intended for Pleasure*, 114.
8. Penner, *The Gift of Sex*, 286.
9. Wheat, *Intended for Pleasure*, 114.
10. Ibid., 121.
11. Penner, *The Gift of Sex*, 204.

Chapter 11: Man to Child

1. Nancy Gibbs, "How Should We Teach Our Children About Sex?" *Time*, 24 May 1993, 63.
2. Ibid., 61.
3. Ibid.

4. Ibid., 62.
5. Clifford and Joyce Penner, *Sex Facts for the Family* (Dallas: Word, 1992), 145.
6. Ibid., 139.
7. Gordon Dalbey, *Father and Son* (Nashville: Nelson, 1992), 58.
8. Ibid., 63.
9. Jane Myers Drew, *Where Were You When I Needed You, Dad?* (Newport Beach, Calif.: Tiger Lily, 1992), 166.
10. Ibid., 93.
11. Richard Butman "Hidden Victims: The Facts About Incest," *His*, April 1983, as cited in Karen B. Mains, *Abuse in the Family* (Elgin, Ill.: Cook, 1987), 23. My experience as a marriage counselor also supports this conclusion.
12. Stanton L. and Brenna B. Jones, *How & When to Tell Your Kids About Sex* (Colorado Springs: NavPress, 1993), 62.

Chapter 12: Man to Woman

1. Bernie Zilbergeld, *The New Male Sexuality* (New York: Bantam, 1992), 162–170.
2. Clifford and Joyce Penner, *Restoring the Pleasure* (Dallas: Word, 1993), 24–25.

Moody Press, a ministry of the Moody Bible Institute,
is designed for education, evangelization, and edification.
If we may assist you in knowing more about Christ
and the Christian life, please write us without obligation:
Moody Press, c/o MLM, Chicago, Illinois 60610.